'*Sex, Drugs and Asperger's Syndrome* is one of my favourite books this year. Luke Jackson provides the reader with an in-depth understanding of many relevant issues regarding both Asperger's Syndrome as well as autism in general. This includes employment, bullying, sexuality, relationships, and much more. The autism community and society as a whole will benefit greatly from these much-needed discussions.'

– Stephen M. Edelson, Ph.D., Executive Director, Autism Research Institute (autism.com), San Diego, California

'With wisdom beyond his years and the mastery of an expressionist artist, Luke guides the reader through the rocky shoals of successful transition from adolescence to adulthood as a person on the autism spectrum. A straightforward, honest must-read for anyone seeking greater understanding of the coming of age of the human soul, autistic or otherwise.'

– Stephen Mark Shore, Ed.D., Clinical Assistant Professor of Special Education at Adelphi University

'Reading *Sex, Drugs and Asperger's Syndrome* feels like having a conversation with an older brother or cousin. He advises without preaching, explains without boring and throws in enough jokes to make the entire reading experience thoroughly enjoyable... From bullying to drugs, employment to nights out, and mental health to sex, it includes the entire spectrum of life without judgement, leaving no stone unturned and rendering no subject taboo... Powerful, honest, funny and friendly, *Sex, Drugs and Asperger's Syndrome* is a must-read.'

– *Penny Gotch,* Disability Now

Sᴇx, ᴅʀUᴳS ᴀɴᴅ Aꜱᴘᴇʀɢᴇʀ'ꜱ SYɴᴅRᴏᴍᴇ

(ASD)

A USER GUIDE TO ADULTHOOD

Luke Jackson

Foreword by Tony Attwood

Jessica Kingsley *Publishers*
London and Philadelphia

First published in hardback in 2016
Paperback edition first published in 2017
by Jessica Kingsley Publishers
73 Collier Street
London N1 9BE, UK
and
400 Market Street, Suite 400
Philadelphia, PA 19106, USA

www.jkp.com

Library of Congress Cataloging in Publication Data
A CIP catalog record for this book is available from the Library of Congress

British Library Cataloguing in Publication Data
A CIP catalogue record for this book is available from the British Library

ISBN 978 1 78592 196 4
eISBN 978 1 78450 139 6

Printed and bound in the United States

CONTENTS

FOREWORD

Those who have read *Freaks, Geeks and Asperger's Syndrome* may have wondered what happened to Luke during his later teenage years and in his early twenties, and those who have not read his first book may be wondering, 'Who is Luke Jackson?' Luke is a brave and eloquent young man who has Asperger's Syndrome, and his autobiographical sequel describes his experiences, reflections and wisdom as he matures from a young teenager into an adult. Luke has become a mentor to those who have Asperger's Syndrome, as well as their parents and other family members. His insights and practical suggestions will also be valued by psychologists who specialise in teenagers and young adults with an autism spectrum disorder (ASD).

Luke describes his recent experiences in a wide range of areas: sensory sensitivity, mental health and especially depression, peer pressure and socialising, being bullied, drugs and addiction, and intimate relationships. The title of his book is perhaps provocative, but the themes are very important to those who have Asperger's Syndrome.

Clinicians and academics are only just starting to appreciate and evaluate the sensory processing profile of those who have an ASD. However, we do know that this characteristic causes considerable distress and that sensory sensitivity tends to be a life-long concern. Fortunately, clinical experience and autobiographies suggest that adults with an ASD have opportunities that they did not have as children to create and maintain an environment and lifestyle that minimises the circumstances that engender aversive sensory experiences. Greater maturity also enables the person to temporarily endure the sensations, rather than yielding to the irresistible urge to escape from them.

Those who do not have an ASD may assume that repeated exposure over many years to an unpleasant sensory experience will eventually achieve habituation, such that the experience is perceived as less intense. They may also advise just trying to ignore the sensation. However, repeated exposure, even over decades, rarely leads to habituation, and it is almost impossible for those who have an ASD to ignore the sensation or find a distracting activity. The person with an ASD needs compassion and cooperation to help either avoid, or momentarily tolerate, intensely aversive sensory experiences. Luke describes sensory sensitivity as occurring throughout the sensory system, from auditory to somatosensory, and the effects of such sensitivity on everyday life.

We know that there is an association between ASD and mental health issues, especially anxiety disorders and depression. Luke focuses primarily on depression, which has occurred regularly throughout his life. There are many reasons why those who have an ASD are more vulnerable to feeling sad and depressed. These include intense feelings of social isolation, alienation and loneliness, self-esteem being based on the criticisms, rather than compliments, of peers, the mental and emotional exhaustion from socialising, coping with change and the unexpected, and difficulties with the organisational aspects of life. There can also be a cognitive style that over-focuses on what could go wrong, or on making a mistake, which leads to a pessimistic outlook on life. Another potential cause of depression is the perception of a diagnosis of Asperger's Syndrome as a disability rather than a difference, and a self-perception of being irreparably defective and eternally socially stupid.

Unfortunately, there are also characteristics of ASD that can prolong the duration and increase the intensity of depression. People who have an ASD have considerable difficulty conceptualising and disclosing in conversation with others their inner thoughts and feelings, preferring to retreat into silent solitude and resolve the feelings of sadness or despair by subjective thought. They may use their special interest as a thought blocker, and as a source of pleasure and restoration of energy that has been depleted throughout the day. Other people are better at articulating and disclosing their feelings to each other. They know that another person can provide a more objective opinion and validation of emotions, and can cheer them up by reassurance and words and gestures of affection or compassion. Family members and friends can provide distraction by initiating enjoyable social experiences, or using humour. In contrast, those who have an ASD can have considerable difficulty resonating with, or being infused by, the happiness of others, and may not perceive social experiences as an antidote to feelings of depression. Indeed, social interactions may reinforce their reasons for feeling depressed by being a reminder of their social clumsiness and confusion. Luke's descriptions of and insight into the area of mental health will be comforting for those who have an ASD, but his advice will also have more credibility, as he has shared their experiences and thoughts.

Peer pressure is an important aspect of late adolescence and Luke describes the various types of peer pressure and strategies to resist encouragement to engage in activities that are unwise and even dangerous. He also describes his experiences as a young adult going out in a group in the evening. Parents are often concerned how their son or daughter with an ASD will be perceived by others, perhaps as a source of malicious fun or worse. The young adult with an ASD is often very brave in wanting to achieve a social life and make new friends, but when this goes wrong or seems unachievable, it is easy to understand how it becomes one of the reasons for remaining a hermit at home.

Another reason for becoming a hermit is being a victim of bullying, and Luke has experienced considerable bullying in his life, which did not stop when he graduated from high-school. Bullying, teasing, and rejection as well as humiliation, can be life-long experiences for those who have an ASD. There may be confusion and despair as to why someone would actually enjoy causing distress to a person who is basically kind, innocuous and inoffensive. There are several reasons that those with an ASD are perceived as easy victims for such behaviours. These include the fact that they are often alone and not with a protective group of friends. Very often they have low self-esteem and low social status and their posture and body language are those of someone who is insecure and vulnerable.

The long-term psychological effects of bullying are devastating. For adolescents who have an ASD, it is a major cause of school refusal and school suspension, often because the victim has become angry and reluctantly retaliated. It can also be a contributory factor in the development of an anxiety disorder, due to constant fear of a bullying 'attack' or ambush each day. Knowing that there is no way to prevent such painful emotional experiences contributes to feelings of hopelessness and depression. The derogatory and provocative comments and actions may also be internalised and eventually believed by the victim, further contributing to low self-esteem and a clinical depression. Thus, the effects of bullying go deeper and last longer for those with an ASD.

Mature adults who have Asperger's Syndrome often replay in their mind instances of being bullied at school or work in order to decipher why they were chosen as a victim, and why someone would be so cruel and malicious. Thus, the event is frequently revisited and is a psychological wound that has never healed. Luke addresses this issue by explaining the motives of predators, which goes some way to assist the reader in achieving closure. He offers strategies to help reduce the harmful effects on self-esteem and the secondary consequences, such as an increase in anxiety and depression. His words are wise.

In our modern society, alcohol and drugs are more available than ever before. Research and my own clinical experience would suggest that between 10 and 30 per cent of patients at drug and alcohol treatment and rehabilitation services have the characteristics of Asperger's Syndrome. Why would those who have an ASD choose the path of addiction in their later adolescence or young adult years?

There are many reasons. The pathway usually starts with access to alcohol – a socially acceptable, but very potent, drug. For the person who has Asperger's Syndrome, alcohol can initially appear to remove the barriers of social inhibition and facilitate social cohesion and inclusion. Alcohol can also reduce social anxiety and the fear of making a social faux pas. It can facilitate the creation of a new, more popular character, and provides a sense of emotional detachment and imperviousness to derogatory remarks. It creates an emotional shield or protective 'bubble', as well as the possibility of inclusion and acceptance in a marginalised peer group of fellow alcohol and drug users.

The next stage can be to experiment with a range of illegal drugs and prescription medication, potentially leading to an addiction. The consequences of intoxication can include being less able to access the frontal lobes, or the thinking and planning areas of the brain, and increased difficulties processing social information, which actually amplifies the central characteristic of ASD. With reduced frontal lobe abilities, the person may also make impulsive or unwise decisions, leading to risky behaviour. There is also the possibility of being in conflict with the law and entering the criminal justice system. In addition, most recreational drugs, such as alcohol and marijuana, directly contribute to the biochemistry and thought processes associated with depression. Luke provides wise advice on this topic, and I hope that his second autobiography will help those with ASD choose a different path than intoxication with the risk of addiction.

Luke also describes aspects of dating, sex and intimate relationships. The ultimate challenge for someone with an ASD is to experience an intimate and lasting relationship. So many subtle and complex abilities are needed to succeed at the dating and relationship game, from recognising the signs of mutual attraction, to the communication and experience of emotional, conversational and physical intimacy. Those who have an ASD often have their first romantic experience several years after their peers. When it does occur, there may be a number of problems, ranging from difficulties reading the body language of mutual attraction, confusion regarding social and sexual conventions and boundaries in a relationship, to aspects of sensory sensitivity that may affect sexual intimacy. Luke provides wise advice on all of this, and creates some interesting metaphors along the way: 'Girls are not vending machines – you don't put kindness in to get sex out.'

Tony Attwood
Minds & Hearts Clinic
Brisbane

ACKNOWLEDGEMENTS

The idea of giving thanks is a strange one. There are not many things in life that, when given, need nothing to be given or taken in return, but gratuity is one. So, to the people listed here, I give my heartfelt thanks for all that you've done for me.

- To my family – wherever they may be at the time, following that spirit of adventure that is such a trademark of the Jackson name, know this: however far away from each other we may be, we'll always be close. There are no trials or tribulations that can break the bonds we all share. Take this acknowledgement as both gratitude for your being there, and as a promise that I'll do the same for you in the future.

- To my friends – you wonderful, acquiescent bunch, you. You take on my eccentricities and completely accept them. There for me through thick and thin, you lot are my rock, and since I can't think of any better way to thank you all, this little note will have to do.

- To Sam, in particular – been through some rough times and many more good, and you've motivated me to get my arse in gear through both. Thanks for the times past, and here's to many more beverages consumed, and to many more adventures had.

- Finally, to every single amazing person I've met within the autism community – without you all, this book wouldn't ever have come to fruition, and I wouldn't be who I am today.

1
INTRODUCTION

MY NAME IS LUKE JACKSON. At present, I am 26 years young, or old. Personally, I've always noted the difference between people who mark themselves in terms of 'years old' or 'years young'. You could draw ties between that and the 'glass half full' paradigm – viewing life in the years that have already passed or in terms of how young you are. Me, I'm neither an optimist nor a pessimist, but a realist, so suffice it to say that 26 years of life have passed.

When I was younger, I wrote a book called *Freaks, Geeks and Asperger Syndrome: A User Guide to Adolescence*. It was a guidebook to the pitfalls of becoming a teenager. I was 13 years old then, and much has happened since. Back then, I was a fresh-faced just-turned-teen, and teenage life was still new, ish. So much has happened since then, and not just on a personal level. Revolutions have come and gone, corporations have risen and fallen and technology has come on in leaps and bounds. Let's face it, the 21st century, so far, has shown itself to be an equally exciting and scary time to be alive.

As a 13-year-old child, nothing I wrote in the prequel to this book could have prepared me for the years that followed. To say it was a rollercoaster ride is like saying the sun is a 'bit warm', or denoting the speed of light as 'pretty fast'. My having come through the other side is the reason for writing this book (which, by the way, I hope you have bought and aren't just reading in the bookshop. If you are, then buy it! It gets better, trust me).

Whenever I speak at conferences, I very often get a resounding 'Wow, you look so different!' Well yes, an entire lifetime's worth of ageing will do that to a person. I do look different to the spikey-haired, beardless wonder on the back of *Freaks, Geeks and Asperger Syndrome*. For starters, I have a lot more hair at the moment, a side-effect of a penchant for rock and metal music, I suppose. It's brown now, but it doesn't tend to stay one colour for very long – if it's on the visible light spectrum, it's a colour my hair has been dyed at one point. Jeans and t-shirts are my staple, though the occasional pair of board shorts or three-quarter length trousers make an appearance every now and then. To sum up the way I look, it's like a surfer born in a part of the world where most of the biggest waves tend to fall from the sky in the form of rain. I have tattoos on my arms, which I spent a long time drawing and designing – graphic design has long been a passion of mine, and my arms are a testament to a love for all things drawn, designed and crafted.

I have green eyes, blue or grey sometimes. They have a habit of changing depending on the situation. I'm still not sure which situations adhere to which eye colours, but life has its mysteries. They lie somewhere above a face largely taken over by a beard that lives there in the winter and goes on hiatus during the summer months. That's pretty much it, other than that I was diagnosed with Asperger's Syndrome when I was younger and have lived with it since.

MEET THE FAMILY

Let me first say that as one of eight children, I was never going to find this sub-chapter a difficult one to write. At the very least, I have eight sentences before I even start to go into detail.

We are a strange family unit, wrought with idiosyncrasies and oddities. The one striking factor is that even though there are eight of us, we're all so different. How that happened, I'm not too sure, but I think it was a conscious effort from everyone. While I cannot speak for the others, for me there was always an abject fear of a loss of individuality. Nowadays, the idea of that is ironic – one of the big pros of autism is that standing out in a crowd has always been easy somehow.

For the purpose of ease of reading, I'm going to introduce everyone in chronological order. This makes sense both in terms of fluidity and because that's how life works – our lives are simply a series of events in chronological order.

Matthew is my oldest brother. He's 30, is 6 foot 5 inches and has size 12 feet. This alone isn't exactly extraordinary information, but the fact that he was one of the youngest babies to be born in Britain, at 24 weeks' gestation, is. Born weighing in at less than a pound, his chances of survival were hit and miss, but survive he did. After missing some developmental milestones, and exhibiting problems in both communicational and social fields, Matthew was diagnosed with dyspraxia and PDD-NOS (pervasive developmental disorder not otherwise specified). (This, back then, was basically autism without all the diagnostic criteria boxes ticked.) After struggling through school, he was later diagnosed as dyslexic. It shows how much things have progressed when you consider that this man, who struggled to make it through his GCSEs because of his dyslexia, now works as an administrator for the Ministry of Defence.

Rachel is 29 years old and a law unto herself – she is confident in her abilities and uses this confidence to achieve her goals. She's fiercely artistic and incredibly social. If I'm honest, Rachel was something of a 'social template' for me growing up; I learned a lot from her about social norms, communication and making friends. Not all of it was right, but it certainly helped.

Sarah is 27 years old and is one of the most interesting people I know. A natural linguist, Sarah completed a degree in French Language, living in France for two years before moving to Spain and pretty much picking up that language in about a week. She is now an accomplished polyglot, fluent in French and Spanish. Every now and again she'll forget English words for things, which is, frankly, hilarious. She was diagnosed with Asperger's Syndrome and auditory processing disorder during her degree; she had problems with the oral exam, as it took her longer to process the words. It became necessary to repeat the sentence one or two times, and a diagnosis was needed to warrant this.

Anna is 22 and is something of a kindred spirit to me. At a young age, me and Anna were very close and then drifted apart slightly before becoming close again. This seems to be a periodic shift – we share the same spirit of adventure, and she will sometimes spend months, even years, away. When we're reunited, however, we always seem to simply pick up where we left off. While there were of course exceptions, since we were siblings, Anna was very tolerant as we grew up. She took a pretty solid stance when it came to people's views on the boys growing up with autism. This was somewhere along the lines of, if anyone was going to call us weird it was *her,* and woe betide anyone outside the family unit who tried to do the same. Anna grew up to become involved in care work, taking the empathy that created the connection we had growing up and putting it to use.

One of the toughest parts of writing this chapter has been maintaining some degree of impartiality, and this is very much the case with Joe. Growing up with Joe was difficult – early on, it was noted that Joe had 'an attention deficit with hyperactive tendencies', and later on he was officially diagnosed with attention deficit hyperactivity disorder (ADHD) and autism with comorbidities. He had a lack of respect for possessions, born of a personal disinterest with them coupled with a lack of the theory of mind to realise that other people may feel differently. Now, Joe is very different – a more empathetic side has flourished, whereas his apathetic side has diminished somewhat.

Ben is now 17 and could not be any more different from the non-verbal, severely autistic child he was in past years. Born very prematurely, Ben was diagnosed as autistic with cerebral palsy very early on. There was little chance of him ever being able to walk, but with almost superhuman effort from both him and mum, using exercises from a regime called the Bobath programme, he has been able to in recent years.

Izaac is six years old and is already one of the cleverest people I know. Absorbing information like a sponge, he has a thirst for knowledge above all else. He has no official diagnosis of Asperger's or autism, but he does have some traits.

Finally, we have Jacqui, my mother and the glue that holds the family together. Somewhat eccentric herself (not pointing the finger here, but genetics has a lot to account for in terms of our idiosyncrasies), she has worked tirelessly to provide for us all over the years, and for this I shall spare her by not giving her actual age.

A LAYMAN'S GUIDE TO ASPERGER'S

Asperger's Syndrome (AS) is, to some degree, still shrouded in mystery. It is a form of autism that is comprised of something called the triad of impairments – communication, social interaction, and theory of mind – and falls under the umbrella of the autism spectrum. Often, repetitive and obsessive behaviour falls under the diagnostic criteria of Asperger's Syndrome and autism, but is not always present in people with an autism spectrum disorder (ASD). Problems with communication and social interaction manifest in a myriad of forms.

I'm often told that you wouldn't know I have Asperger's to look at me. I've had a quarter of a century to craft my front, and the art of 'pretending to be normal' is something that I have finely tuned over the years. However, even though I look pretty normal (at least in a Hell's Angels kind of way), the quirks start to show when you dig a little deeper. My hair is long because I can't stand having my hair cut. The whole process of cutting hair is completely fine, but backwashes, those demonic contraptions meant for washing hair in hairdressers, are just too much. The shampoo smells too strong, the awkward accidental eye contact is terrible, I hate people touching my scalp and I loathe having my neck touched.

The jeans and t-shirt seem innocuous enough, but only once I've actually bought them. Navigating rows of t-shirts, feeling through till I get the right one, is nothing short of a pain. As for jeans...I am a 31-inch leg, size 33-inch waist. Ish. Finding ones that fit exactly, that are made of the right material, not too scratchy, not too soft...the whole process very soon becomes a military operation.

I dye my hair to stand out, fine. However, the reason behind this is that if I look a little different, I find it a lot easier to come across as 'eccentric' when I make one of the inevitable social faux pas that go hand in hand with Asperger's. If people chalk any discrepancies in behaviour down to an innocent streak of oddness as opposed to Asperger's, I have a 'margin for error' when it comes to social prerogative. The bonus lies in the fact that I still don't get talked down to and if anything goes seriously wrong, I can still 'let the cat out of the bag' so to speak. I suppose the root of the matter is that I still have a fall-back should I need it.

The tattoos? Each tattoo on my arm pertains to a different expression or idiom. So far I have 'Don't judge a book by its cover', 'Storm in a teacup', 'Fuel to the fire', 'Heard it through the grapevine' and 'See no evil, hear no evil, speak no evil.'

While we have diagnostic criteria for the diagnosis of Asperger's Syndrome and autism spectrum disorders, the traits vary wildly from person to person. A diagnosis of Asperger's Syndrome can, and often does, take years. The reason for this is that even the traits that seem watertight can manifest differently in different people.

For example, people with AS are known to have problems with eye contact. The kicker here is that it can be in very different ways. My little brother Joe, who was diagnosed with autism and ADHD, had very good eye contact in a sense. The problem was that it was inappropriate – he had to be way up close and staring right into the eyes of the person he was conversing with, regardless of how well he knew them. I maintain pretty decent eye contact when I first meet someone, which tends to become more hit and miss as I get to know them, in that I feel more comfortable being myself. As soon as conversation transcends the boundaries of 'small talk', however, eye contact nigh on disappears and I turn into Mr Autistic. To look into someone's eyes in this situation, be it an argument, enquiry into the well-being of a family member, or anything at all that goes beyond 'Hello, how are you', is painful.

Social situations are more complex, and how people deal with these varies from person to person. Some people fare better in certain situations than others, and some people develop with age, finding personal ways to cope with their weak points. Personally, when I found out I had Asperger's, the diagnostic criteria became a list of challenges. Because I'd always had problems with crowds, I booked a gig to push myself a little further. I went to parties. Eleanor Roosevelt said that people should do one thing each day that scares them – for people with autism, this can often be as simple as a walk to the shops.

So much has happened since my diagnosis, both in and outside the world of autism; the most notable thing, of course, has to be the change that makes the title of this book medically incorrect in the USA – the reclassification of Asperger's Syndrome by the American Psychological Association's *DSM-5 Handbook* in 2013, under the umbrella term 'autism spectrum disorder'. This is hardly the right place to vent on the subject, but suffice it to say that this certainly seems to make life a lot easier for the people classifying Asperger's than it does for the people with it – sorry, with an autism spectrum disorder, or on the autism spectrum. Or something.

One of the things I hear constantly in terms of Asperger's Syndrome, is: 'You wouldn't notice' or 'I wouldn't have guessed.' Now, this is kind of a double-edged sword here, one side positive and one negative. (Obviously, in terms of a double-edged sword, both sides are negative. Let's face it, it's a sword – you're not going to decapitate someone with one side and chop carrots with the other. But I digress.)

On one side of this 'sword of pretence', you have achieved a kind of nirvana in terms of normality. You have become so honed at suppressing your little 'idiosyncrasies' that they have all but disappeared to the untrained eye. Congratulations, have a cookie. I mean it, this can be a great thing; sometimes simply coming across as a little eccentric as opposed to full-blown Asperger's does have its uses.

Every up comes with a down, however, and this situation is exactly the same. We have a phrase denoting 'pretending to be normal' in our family; we call it 'running an emulator'. Now, if you'll permit me, I'm going to explain why this is a problem, and this is going to get a bit geeky. If you won't permit me, then I can only apologise, because I'm going to happily plod on anyway.

An emulator is a form of software that tries to mimic one platform on another, using a complicated system of code and prioritising of hardware. For example, you could run an emulator on a PC in order to run console games. The thing is, these don't tend to work so well – they get the job done, sure, but they're just not purpose-built. It's rather like cooking toast on a bonfire – you can make it work, but it would be a damn sight easier just to use a toaster.

Part of the reason for this is that certain machines are built for certain things. There are a multitude of things that people on the spectrum are good at doing, but the crux of the matter is that we are all human. The nature of humans, including people with ASD, is that we come with an inbuilt instinct for survival and to some extent, betterment, if that means the furthering of the species in general. Every person has their own strengths and weaknesses; this is what makes us human, with all our flaws. I am in no way saying that everything when it comes to autism is a trade-off – it isn't. Unfortunately, some people on the spectrum can be lacking in social and communicational skills, and yet still not be able to paint like Picasso or count cards like the Rain Man. It is a matter of personal grievance that throughout the course of my diagnosis I failed to develop any savant-like abilities and/or near photographic powers of recollection as was expected of me.

When I wrote the precursor to this book, *Freaks, Geeks and Asperger Syndrome*, which is, in essence, this book's *raison d'être*. I was fresh faced, bushy tailed... I struggle to think of another expression to tag to the end of this, but I'm sure there is one. The point is, I was 13 years old – I was very young, and have now lived twice as long as I had then. I have literally had a lifetime of experience since then, and to read back through what I wrote at that time renders me incredulous – I was a different person.

Since then, I have struggled with a myriad of issues, been through the darkest of times, come through the highest of highs and the lowest of lows, but the point is, I'm still here. Unfortunately, suicidal ideation in adults with Asperger's Syndrome is high. A study in June 2014 revealed that 66 per cent of 374 adults with AS had had suicidal thoughts at some point, and 35 per cent had actually tried to commit suicide.[1] The study is a relevant one – even on a personal level I wasn't sure whether I'd be here at this point in time. So, if this book stops some people along the way from making some of the mistakes I did, and helps some people out of the sticky situations I got into, then it has done its job, and that will be worth a hundred bad reviews.

Part of surviving with autism and Asperger's Syndrome is learning to deal with the differences, the things that single you out from others, and turning those into your strengths. In the modern world, with its competitive ethos, the hustle and bustle of the social and work environment, and fast-paced lifestyles, everyone is constantly trying to find ways to stand out from the crowd. Chances are, if you're on the autism spectrum, then that may come easily to you.

One of the problems with looking in on Asperger's is that even when everything looks normal, a lot of things are internalised, and dealt with accordingly. For example, I still have to sit with my back to the wall, and before I sit down I still have to walk around a place to look for the exits, and I could go on. These are things that just go unnoticed in day-to-day conversation, but if I'm not permitted to do these things, at worst I'll 'meltdown'; at best, it's like pushing a big 'pause' button on life. I can't think, I can't concentrate and I can't work. I can't really do much of anything until it's resolved.

---

1   Cassidy, S., Bradley, P., Robinson, J., Allison, C., McHugh, M. and Baron-Cohen, S. (2014) 'Suicidal ideation and suicide plans or attempts in adults with Asperger's Syndrome attending a specialist diagnostic clinic: a clinical cohort study.' *The Lancet Psychiatry* 1, 2, 142–147.

SENSORY ISSUES AND AUTISM

The senses of people with an ASD are often more keenly tuned to outside stimuli, and more sensitive to their effects. Sounds can be louder, smells almost omnipresent. There are still certain shops I cannot walk past without holding my nose – and as walking past shops holding your nose kind of makes people around you feel insecure, there are certain shops I can't walk past full stop. I still cannot walk round supermarkets for too long, as the flickering lights give me a headache. Social situations and certain crowds cause almost crippling anxiety. Unannounced physical contact, I react almost comically to – my little brother in particular knows to jump back when he taps me on the shoulder lest he's caught by an all-too-literal knee-jerk reaction.

As humans, we are sensory creatures; our entire perception of the world is made up of a conglomerate of signals sent from various organs to the brain. As we walk down the street, we see our surroundings and judge distances from obstacles accordingly, and we keep track of our position in space using obstacles like walls or the edge of the pavement as markers. As our feet hit the floor, we feel the ground against the soles of our feet; our brain knows how softly or hard to tread so as not to damage our feet, and we use feedback from both sight and touch to navigate the terrain. We use our sense of smell to track food, and it can be used to find a potential mate – think of how cologne works; we are still animalistic in that sense. Hearing can be used to engage in conversation with peers or to listen out for potential predators (though I'm not sure the average drunk on a Saturday night looking for a fight constitutes a 'predator'!). Our sense of taste was originally to lead us to foods that were nutritionally beneficial to us, and away from foods that could be poisonous or harmful.

Senses don't just work on an 'on/off' basis. The best indicator of this is the subject of pain thresholds. Different people can take different levels of pain, but what one person finds unbearable, another may find almost painless, even relaxing.

These senses are important to us. More and more, we're developing ways to make the world accessible to people who have lost one or more of these senses, and sometimes even to replace them. What happens, though, when these senses start not failing, but malfunctioning? An example of how senses can malfunction is misophonia, where a noise that's almost imperceptible to one person may be incredibly loud and irritating to the sufferer. This noise can be seemingly innocuous, such as someone eating or even breathing, but it can be enough to send some people into a fervour. This is in no way intrinsically linked with autism, but it is by no means the only sense that can misfire.

The sensory problems associated with autism spectrum disorders are awkward and difficult at best, and debilitating at worst. They can affect all areas of life, from social life (yes, we do have one!) to relationships. They can be an absolute pain in the backside and, if you let them, they can rule your whole life. I wear clothes under sufferance now, but when I was younger I used to detest the feel of most fabrics. Both I and my little brother Ben have lived in a dressing gown for pretty much our entire lives. (Just to clarify, I don't mean literally lived in a dressing gown, I mean that we wore it most of the time while growing up.) To this day, when I'm picking clothes to wear, I don't look at anything, I just run my fingers over the clothes on the hangers until I touch something I like the feeling of.

Rather than making you trawl through paragraphs and paragraphs on the seven types of sensory input, I'm going to put them in bullet point form, because I'm nice like that. Included with each one is a little information on how these can 'misfire' or become extremely sensitive for people on the autism spectrum.

- **Olfactory (smell):** Our sense of smell is extremely important, and I only realised how important after I met a few people who were anosmic. Our sense of smell dictates a number of things in life; it can signal familiarity with a person, and various people can be recognised by smell alone. In fact, some people use this as a marker of individuality and will actively wear a certain perfume that they've appropriated as 'their smell'.

  Let's face it, smells are great, and as someone on the autism spectrum I have a pretty highly tuned nose. I've developed an affinity for cooking in recent years and I'm not bad at it, partly because I can pick out flavours separately by smell and work out what's missing. However, having a hyper-effective sense of smell carries with it disadvantages. The world is a maze of smells, and simply walking around can be like running an olfactory gauntlet. I have to know where I live well, because I have to memorise routes that will avoid certain shops or stalls. Body odour is an ever-present problem, and not just because of people with traditional 'body odour' as it's normally portrayed. The thing is, everyone has body odour. Literally everyone. It's part of being human; but when you perceive these smells constantly, the world becomes a very sensory place, and sometimes not in a good way.

While hypersensitivity to smell is one thing, often people with an ASD can experience the other side of things – olfactory hyposensitivity – and that can be just as problematic. Our sense of smell, while less integral to our survival than it would have been in times past, is still pretty important. We use it to tell whether food is burning or has 'gone off', and we even use it as a yardstick for our own personal hygiene. (I still smell my clothes to see whether they're clean before I put them in the wash. That's bad, isn't it? Forget I said that.) The thing is, without our sense of smell, it's easy to miss these things. It can be more difficult to identify body odour, for example, and this can lead to a lack of showering and personal hygiene in people with autism. This is when things like showering are problematic anyway (but we'll get onto that in a bit more detail a little later).

- **Auditory (sound):** Sound, to me, is one of the worst and best senses in the world. A self-confessed audiophile, I love my music, and I love that I can pick out different instruments and riffs within the music I listen to. It adds a whole other level to the music, and I'm highly thankful for it. While it's difficult to tell because we all hear differently, both in terms of volume, and pitch and tone, I don't have too many problems with auditory hypersensitivity. I hear much better in my left ear, so do end up turning my head to the side when I'm listening intently, but on a personal level my hypersensitivity to sound has calmed down a lot since I was younger.

  There are so many levels to the problems auditory perception difficulties can cause that it isn't appropriate simply to group them into hypersensitivity and hyposensitivity. Often the body can misfire and interpret a volume or pitch as higher or lower than it is. In this case, seemingly incongruous sounds in the background, such as the high-pitched whine of a television or the hum of an air conditioning unit can be distracting at best, and infuriating or painful at worst. In school this was a huge problem: school was a mess of unfamiliar sounds – school bells, chairs creaking and squeaking, and children running through corridors. Worse, the teachers would talk and then suddenly up the volume to shout at someone who was talking in class, without so much as a moment's warning. By nature, people on the autism spectrum have a higher startle reflex than other people – their fight-or-flight reflex is more keenly attuned. This can mean that sudden changes in volume can be daunting and can seriously disturb concentration (a real problem in the school or workplace) or even cause a meltdown.

Problems can be caused with how sounds are perceived too, not just the level they are perceived at. This can be an issue both in terms of concentration and attentiveness, or in determining the origin of different sounds. My (not so) little brother Joe, who has ADHD, has problems determining when someone is talking to him; this is rooted in an inability to properly distinguish background noise from foreground noise. In the past, this resulted in numerous people accusing him of ignoring them, but all it took to get his attention was to use his name as a precursor at the start of a sentence. It was only a slight change, but it made all the difference. Another strange anomaly in terms of hearing for a person with AS is an inability to distinguish where a noise is coming from, which can be worse in places with a lot of background noise. This doesn't sound like much of an issue, and most of the time it isn't, but when you can't distinguish who is speaking in a conversation involving several people, it can be problematic. Another example is someone knocking at a front door – a knocking sound that sounds as if it comes from the back of the house just makes you wonder what fell over, and doesn't exactly inspire you to go and answer the door. To combat this in my house, we have a proximity infrared detector that goes off with a certain sound whenever someone is outside the door. That way, judging the direction of the sound is not a problem, as the noise is unique. This is a slightly high-tech way of dealing with this issue, but doorbells with specific sounds work too!

- **Gustatory (taste):** Taste is difficult when it comes to autism. Theorised as an evolutionary throwback to help us determine what was good for us when our species was in its infancy, it's now the cornerstone of all things culinary. Now, far from simply signifying foods that are good for us or poisonous to us, taste is integral to our sense of enjoyment when it comes to food. As you can probably guess from the last couple sentences, I love my food and, more specifically, I love to cook. When taste is hyposensitive or hypersensitive, or misfires entirely, it renders this gastronomic world nigh on impossible to enjoy.

  When a person is hypersensitive, certain tastes can be impossible to stomach, and even the slightest contact with foods of a certain taste or texture can be enough to induce vomiting, or the mere thought of them can induce nausea. This is far from simply causing slight nausea or discomfort – when I was younger, the taste of vinegar, for example, was enough to cause vomiting and actual physical pain. At best, this kind of gustatory hypersensitivity can make certain foods and textures no-go zones; at worst, it can make a person's diet highly restrictive, and be difficult for them to obtain the right level of nutrients needed for good health.

Hyposensitivity is an entirely different matter, yet can cause the same amount of impairment as hypersensitivity. Hyposensitivity carries with it some other complications, however, such as pica. Pica is the habit of eating non-foodstuffs such as grass, soil or sand – basically, things with highly varied textures and tastes. In the case of pica, the person can sometimes be searching for something missing nutritionally from their diet.

When he was younger, my little brother Ben used to lick things. The objects would tend to be metallic, such as chair legs and railings, and sometimes he would eat coins. Using a mixture of intuition and very fuzzy science, we added zinc to his diet, and the pica died down. While there are much, much better ways to work things out than this, and while this is not the sole cause of pica it may be something to look out for. Otherwise, pica can often be caused by someone searching for sensory stimulation, and sensory toys or equipment can help. This is not to say you need to trawl through specific sensory magazines looking at overpriced pieces of plastic and felt. Sometimes the best thing to do can simply be to look at what kind of things the person is eating and then replace them with something safer and of a similar texture. It can be remedied with a little thought, though sometimes it can take a bit of creativity as well.

- **Vestibular (balance):** Ah, the vestibular system. That old foe, the system of balance, that which has caused so many spilled drinks, so many minor and major injuries.

I have had much experience with both hypersensitivity and hyposensitivity when it comes to the vestibular system, and any one person isn't necessarily only hyposensitive or hypersensitive – this can vary depending on the situation and environmental variables.

Hyposensitivity in terms of balance is an odd one and is particularly common in those with forms of ADHD/ADD (attention deficit disorder). People may seek extra vestibular input by banging into people, for example – this was the case with my little brother Joe, and was particularly abrasive when you consider that me and my little brother Ben were hypersensitive, and this kind of extra sudden movement was highly uncomfortable, and enough to set off the aforementioned fight-or-flight reflex and trigger some pretty heavy anxiety. Another way hyposensitivity can manifest, and a very common form, is spinning. Spinning, for me, is a great way to concentrate, to get my thoughts in order, but it's still highly misunderstood. When I was younger, I simply did not get dizzy. I was friendly with a boy who had ADHD, and he was the same. We used to play a game called 'dizzy dinosaurs' – the idea was that you spun around on the spot until you became dizzy. However, we didn't get dizzy, so we just spun. We once both got into trouble because someone tried to join in, and after around 20 minutes they fell over and threw up. Now I'm older I get dizzy much more easily, but I still walk in circles to help me concentrate.

Vestibular hypersensitivity is very common in people with ASD and can particularly impair performance in day-to-day life. Our system of balance dictates whether we are 'upright' or not and how far from our normal standing, sitting or lying down position we actually are. For people with a hypersensitive vestibular system, the body can misinterpret physical feedback, so a gentle tap or someone brushing past in the street can knock them completely off-balance. In addition to this, it can take a little while for the vestibular system to 'normalise' when going from moving to stationary, especially quickly, and this can cause problems in many facets of life, in particular car journeys, where car sickness is an ever-present and all-pervasive problem. There are all kinds of potions and remedies for this, from those acupressure wristbands to travel sickness tablets, which have worked in the past for me.

- **Proprioceptive (body positioning):** Problems with proprioceptive input in autism are well documented and are even written into the diagnostic criteria. Anyone who knows someone on the autism spectrum will probably have had some problems with proximity issues; a person seemingly having no knowledge of personal space, and standing too close to them. Be aware, there is a flipside to this – anyone on the autism spectrum reading this will probably have had their train of thought suddenly derailed by someone very pointedly shuffling away or calling them out on 'invasion of their personal space'.

This unknowing personal space invasion (why is this not a video game yet? I see a great sequel to the original game here) is a side-effect of proprioceptive issues that come part and parcel with autism.

I have something a number of people have as a comorbidity of autism spectrum disorder – dyspraxia. A disorder affecting fine and gross motor coordination in children and adults, dyspraxia is also seen in a pretty hefty number of people with ASD (although it's not exclusively given as a diagnosis to those on the autism spectrum). Dyspraxia affects coordination in day-to-day life and means certain tasks, particularly fiddly tasks or things involving mixed coordinated motion such as riding a bike (which I still can't do) or tying shoelaces (which I also still can't do), are particularly difficult or even impossible. On top of this, it can affect planning, time-keeping and organisation skills – in short, it affects all forms of coordination, both mental and physical.

I'm not going to split proprioceptive input into hyposensitivity and hypersensitivity, because proprioceptive difficulties are far more, well, difficult than this. For a person on the autism spectrum the world can be a maze of both visible and invisible boundaries that can be almost impossible to navigate in any sufficient way. Often, coordinating separate parts of the body in unison can be a challenge, so a person may turn their entire body to look at something, or reach across themselves to grab an object instead of using the hand that's nearest.

- **Visual (sight):** It can be hard to explain differences in the visual system from a personal point of view, as discrepancies in sight can be difficult to diagnose and monitor properly. This can be for a number of reasons, but a huge obstacle for me has been clear communication when it comes to eye tests. For example, let's say I go to an optician's. I'm asked to look at some letters through green and red coloured slides. I can read the same amount of letters with both slides, but am then asked which one looks better. This is a tough question: I kind of prefer green to red, but neither of them are my favourite colour, so I go for green. What the specialist means, however, isn't which colour looks better aesthetically, nor is he even talking about the colour specifically. He is asking which coloured lens makes the letters being viewed clearer. The problem isn't one of sight but of communication, and this is often something to watch out for and to take stock of.

  Problems with sight can be an issue in autism though, and these can often vary from people who aren't on the autism spectrum. A great example is flickering when it comes to fluorescent lighting – there is research to show that people on the autism spectrum see at a higher frequency than other people, or have a higher 'flicker fusion threshold'. While certain fluorescent bulbs that put out light at around 100–120 Hz are not usually perceived to be flickering, to me, and to many others, school classrooms and supermarkets in particular become low-budget discos whose only purpose seems to be to cause headaches. They serve this purpose well, because cause headaches they do, both literally and figuratively. As well as causing that deep throbbing headache that it usually takes a couple of bottles of good rum to achieve, they make it damn near impossible to concentrate. As the cost of LED and higher frequency lighting drops, and as new electronic ballasts are produced for tube lighting, this is becoming less of a problem, but it's still there!

The jury is out on the subject of visual impairment in autism. Some research suggests that people with an ASD have greater visual acuity and are able to pick up objects with greater visual clarity than other people, while others believe there is no difference. Recent studies show that more than half the people on the autism spectrum have visual problems. Whether these visual problems are tied in with having an ASD, however, is a different story, and one that may be too complicated to tell.

- **Somatosensory (physical environmental perception):** With no small sense of purpose, I decided to save the best till last here. This sense is so omniscient, so all-pervasive, so intrinsically tied in to all other senses that I felt I had to leave it till last as a conclusion and the sensory knot that binds all the senses together.

    Loosely termed, this sense would be the 'sense of touch'. I have used the somewhat cumbersome phrase 'physical environmental perception' instead, however, as somatosensory input is an umbrella term including touch, feel, hot and cold input and pain response. Somatosensation is basically any sensation interpreted by the skin and certain parts of the body. This is probably the sense most affected when it comes to ASD. Whether someone is hyposensitive or hypersensitive in this area can often depend on the diagnosis. People with ADHD/ADD can often be hyposensitive, seeking extra external pressure and sensation, whereas someone with Asperger's or autism may be hypersensitive, shying away from physical contact and external stimuli.

How these hypersensitivities and hyposensitivities manifest can vary depending on what side of the autism spectrum a person resides. If someone is predominantly ADHD or ADD, they can often be hyposensitive. This means that a person will actively seek out extra-sensory input, such as bumping into other people, bouncing off walls (literally) and binding or crushing themselves under objects. When he was younger, Joe used to lie under the couch cushions and make us all sit on them – it was a great game as kids, but also gave him the extra-sensory stimulation he needed, and we found his hyperactivity would abate slightly for the rest of the day. Now, he's found ways to achieve this effect himself, namely by wearing extra and tight-fitting clothes to gain a similar sensation. This hyposensitivity ties into different aspects of autism, such as insomnia, which affects many people on the autism spectrum. Often, in this scenario, a weighted blanket can be a godsend and can help many people with an ASD who suffer from sleep problems.

Hyposensitivity is a sensory minefield, causing a number of problems that shouldn't be underestimated in their severity. One of the biggest problems of hyposensitivity, and one that can become very dangerous if left unchecked, is the seeming absence or dulling of nociceptive input, or a person's perception of pain. While in theory, this seems great – to attempt death-defying feats without fear of pain-based rebuttal – in practice it is something altogether different.

We are imbued with a sense of pain for a reason; it is our body's way of telling us when something's wrong. If that misfires and our pain threshold is so far through the proverbial roof that a broken arm is akin to a light headache, then it can prevent someone from seeking medical attention when they really need it. This can prove particularly problematic in later life, when, for example, a broken ankle that wasn't set in a cast doesn't heal properly, causing bone deformity or malformation. In situations like this, improper form caused by a past injury when walking or running can cause repeat injury, and a vicious circle can occur.

For some of those with autism, self-harm can be a common issue, and one that isn't always associated with depressive behaviour. Self-harm can become evident in a number of ways – cutting and drug abuse are the obvious forms, but banging one's head against objects, punching walls and purposefully engaging in self-destructive behaviour are others. When it comes to physical pain, hyposensitivity can be a catalyst in terms of self-harm as, like a lot of depressive behaviour-motivated actions, particularly destructive ones, self-harm can often simply be an attempt to feel *something*. In this situation, replacing the negative stimuli with something non-damaging is important. There are a number of interventions to deal with this; an elastic band around the wrist is something that has helped in the past for me, and I still 'ping' a hair tie against my arm sometimes.

Hypersensitivity in terms of the somatosensory system can be just as problematic as hyposensitivity and it is probably a more acknowledged side of the sensory difficulties involved in ASD. The best way to describe hypersensitivity in terms of touch and feel is to liken it to hearing the world with the volume turned all the way up. Everything is jarring, and the more you are subjected to certain sensations, the more painful each frequency becomes. After some time, you may acclimatise, desensitise even, but that still doesn't address the root problem.

Autism is a strange disorder – and it is a disorder. It has its advantages and disadvantages, but things are disordered, a little bit mixed up. This is no more self-evident than when it comes to touch and feel. Someone running their hand over your arm can feel as if someone is digging for oil on your skin, and a slight nudge on the subway can send pain through your entire body. Somatosensory hypersensitivity can cause problems right across the board, from day-to-day life, to friendships and relationships. It feels as if the body isn't able to accurately gauge the pressure or manner in which someone is touching you, and just makes a wild estimate instead. A tight hug from a family member can feel as uncomfortable as being groped by a stranger, while a light touch can feel like being scalded by boiling water. Obviously this has ramifications when it comes to friendships and relationships, and it can sometimes take more adjusting by other people than by the person on the autism spectrum.

Problems with touch and feel extend much further than just human contact. When it comes to clothes, I am immensely picky, and if I don't feel right with what I'm wearing, I simply can't work, can't concentrate, can't think. The dichotomy of disrobing, or the soliloquy of the shirt and trousers, to put an overly poetic twist on things, has been a struggle from day one. Clothes have their advantages and disadvantages: on the one hand, they keep you warm; on the other hand, they're uncomfortable, they itch, they're constricting, you're continuously battling between being too hot and too cold, they rub and you're constantly aware that you've bandaged the vast majority of your body in a plethora of different fabrics. As you can probably discern from the previous sentence, I view clothes as a necessary evil.

Oddly enough though, even with this disdain for the feel of fabrics, I still like fashion, with all its fickle idiosyncrasies. The thing about being autistic, for me, is that I constantly feel as if I'm on the outside looking in - at any social event, I'm just on the fringes. When it comes to fashion, however trivial it sounds, I can express that. I like to dress slightly differently, to mix different sets of trends, and being bipolar as well, I tend to dress to fit my mood. It's just that the process of buying clothing in the first place takes a little longer than it does for other people.

When it comes to clothing and ASD, many people are a mixture of hypersenstive and hyposensitive. As I was growing up, I tended to veer towards loose-fitting clothes, and as I grow older, I feel myself sticking to clothes that hug my shape, rubbing as little as possible when I move. However, one constant that has always remained true is that both me and my little brother Ben have always favoured softer textures, such as cotton and polyester, while my little brother Joe, who has ADHD, has always favoured fabrics like nylon and rough wool. Ben and I have always leaned towards hypersensitivity, and in particular I've always struggled with physical contact, especially light touch, whereas Joe has always tended towards hyposensitivity, seeking extra-sensory input wherever possible.

There are many different interventions that can help with somatosensory issues. The first, and most important one in my eyes, is that there should always be pre-warning before touch that may be uncomfortable. This doesn't always have to be 'I'm going to hug you now' – it's as important that help in these matters is done right as it is that it's done at all. While it isn't always the case, statements like this may come across as condescending and can often insult the ASD person's intelligence. Obviously, behaviour should be adjusted according to the individual, but often simply things like giving due warning, approaching from the front and not hugging for too long can help. Other activities like getting a haircut can be made a lot easier by introducing the different sensations involved gradually – having my hair washed has always been painful, and simply talking to the hairdressers about this, making sure the water is close to room temperature and that they aren't too rough has helped massively. In this case, communication is key.

2

PiTFALLS OF AdOLESCENCE AND BEYOND

BEING A TEENAGER IS HARD. This is a fact of life – there are so many different things happening all at once, and in the middle of it all, you're often still trying to work out exactly 'who you are'. While this sounds a little wishy-washy, I say this with the calm Zen and slightly smug attitude of someone who has come through the other side after very nearly not doing so. Everyone reading this will have or have had a different experience – some easier, some more difficult – but I don't think anyone will disagree that everyone has a tough time at some point or other. If you're reading this and your life was peachy from age 13 to 20, I think I speak for everyone when I say we're all very proud and/or jealous of you and you should go and stand in the corner.

The annoying, and somewhat inconvenient, part of the teenage transition is that everything happens at once. Often the information given to you is not all that helpful, or is at the very least a little understated, even though this has become a bit better over recent years. Growing up, you often hear euphemistic talk of 'getting hair in places you didn't have it before' or 'parts of your body growing' or 'experiencing mood swings as your hormones change'. This is all very nice and fluffy, but what they don't say is that guys can develop a bunch of stretch marks in weeks as muscles grow where there weren't any before, girls' breasts can be sore as hell when they're developing, and that very often your mood can change so fast that you don't know whether you want to have sex, cry, or do both at the same time.

If this is happening to you at the moment, I'm here to tell you there's a pretty high probability that you're going to be okay. Not just that, but you will come through the other side with a new appreciation of the world, in that you will most definitely have weathered some tough times and survived. You'll almost certainly have a healthy dose of cynicism as well, possibly with a side of cynicism. Just go with it, you'll grow to love it, trust me. (NB: I might be being sarcastic.)

An interesting part of growing up as a teenager was the way people's attitudes towards difference changed. There was still a similar distrust in the unknown when it came to certain social set-ups, but things were a little different from school. During school life, everyone had tried very hard to fit in, to make sure they were all listening to the same music, playing the same sports, and watching the same films and media. Once school was over, people were (tentatively) branching out, consuming different media, wearing different things – in short, people were *trying* to be different. Now, I don't know about you, reader, but standing out has never been something I've had a problem with. This was a heady time, I was attending college and, ironically, for the first time in my life I had people that I could relate to. It was odd, finding commonalities in difference, but it was a good feeling. We could be vilified, estranged, but that just cemented the belief that whatever muddled path we were following, we were heading in the right direction, and if we were to be martyred for our quirks along the way, so be it.

Those were simpler and more difficult times, in equal measure, but at the time they were everything to me. In one way, they shaped who I have become today, but in another, I made a hell of a lot of mistakes. Part of the reason for this was at the time, everything meant so much; day-to-day life felt as if I was fighting a battle, and it was very hard to picture the future, or even acknowledge its existence. One thing is nigh on certain though – if I'd given a quick nod and a tip of the hat to 'future me', I would have skipped out on some terrible decisions and very probably set myself up to make things a little easier later on down the line. Since time machines aren't in existence yet, you only get one chance; if you're heading towards teenage years, and you only take one thing from this chapter, let it be that.

UNDER PRESSURE

An extensive, though non-exclusive, type of pressure that teenagers have to deal with on a day-to-day basis is peer pressure. Everyone looks to everyone else for inspiration as to how to be different and still fit in. As everyone walks that fine line between standing out and fitting in, they are often fiercely critical of those who stray from the path.

Insidious and all-pervasive, peer pressure is very difficult to explain. Everyone at some point will have experienced it but it varies in the way it is delivered and in its severity. It doesn't apply only to teenagers, but to everyone.

Put simply, peer pressure is external pressure to dress a certain way, act a certain way, or do certain things that others are doing under the premise of subordination. It is the staring eyes and oppressive silence of a conglomerate of smokers offering a cigarette to a person who has never smoked. It is the sneers of a group scorning someone for dressing differently from them, or having different coloured hair. It is the ridicule of peers putting 'friends' under pressure to engage in sexual activity at younger and younger ages, sometimes because it's either normal to them or because they want to pretend that it's normal to them.

Of course, these are just a few examples of peer pressure, but pressure doesn't just come from peers. Modern media outlets have created a simpler way of using peer pressure to their advantage – magazines and music feed into youth culture, and shape it, and vice versa. It's a symbiotic relationship – one feeds into the other, and both form the basis for teenage culture, be it food, fashion or music. This creates a whole other basis for peer pressure – if you're not on trend, you're simply left behind or ridiculed. This phenomenon isn't documented that well, never mind the tools to guard against it provided. Sure, there are plenty of articles decrying social media as 'the new digital peer pressure', increasing smoking and drinking in teens, but what there isn't a lot of is articles highlighting modern media's influence as negative peer pressure.

All this adds up to a pretty difficult lifestyle for the teenagers of today. They have to dress a certain way, look a certain way, listen to certain music, act a certain way, strike a perfect balance between social life and academic life, while being shunned from most places because they're either too old to be hanging around parks or too young to be in pubs. Let's face it, the tender teenage years are some of the toughest.

Pressure doesn't always come from peers either. Parents can unknowingly apply extra pressure in the form of academic pressure, pressure to socialise, sometimes even pressure to 'be normal'. This can be on purpose or by accident, but can often be the 'tipping point' that makes things too much to cope with. People often see their parents as the last bastion in a world where everything seems pitted against them, and when a parent adds to that pressure it can feel like a huge betrayal.

If there are any parents reading this, it is vitally important that you consider how your actions affect your son or daughter, and how they are likely to react. Teenage behaviour is somewhat elastic – the more pressure you apply, the more you push, and pull, the more resistance there will be in return. In addition to this, if you apply too much pressure, adding to inevitable external weight, the person will snap. Everyone has a breaking point, and there are so many different forms of pressure to contend with – from peers, from the media, from teachers – that parents are often counted as the last line of defence by a child growing into a teenager.

The question about what to do to combat the aforementioned modes of peer pressure needs to be approached from multiple angles.

First and foremost, it's important to note that knowledge is power. As soon as you start to recognise these kinds of peer pressure and the effect they are having on you, they lose a great deal of influence. Often, peer pressure is cumulative in its effect – it is drip-fed through loaded conversations and the actions of others. We fall prey to it without even knowing, through either a desire for acceptance or a fear of reprisal. Examples of peer pressure range from the simple to the complex, from a mock-casual, 'Oh, go on, you know you want to anyway', to even just a well-placed silence or laugh. It is important to recognise what constitutes peer pressure before we even begin to avoid it. I've compiled a list of different types of peer pressure, split into both spoken and unspoken. A word of caution – expect bluntness; tact and subtlety are not my strong points.

SPOKEN PEER PRESSURE

- **Vocalised direct pressure** – *'Go on, you know you want to...'*

    Blunt and brutal, this kind of peer pressure is a type many people have had personal experience with. That dare, that cigarette, that first drink...this is very direct and can be very intimidating when coming from a group of people. Often in this situation, the best option is to be as direct when saying no to the person or people applying the pressure as they are in doing so. It's important not to be aggressive in saying no and not to raise your voice, but simply to refuse, even if that means answering with 'Maybe another time', if that appeases. It may be a lie, but the idea that the timing is simply wrong is only as vacuous as the premise for the pressure being applied.

- **Negative expectation** – *'I expected better of you.'*

Often, not so much from peers, this can come from parents, teachers or other adults and can be just as damaging as other types of pressure. On researching various types of pressure and their effects, I read much on various types of 'positive pressure'. While I fear I may step on a few toes here, I'm going to come out and say it: *there is no such thing.* If you squeeze a balloon hard enough, that balloon will pop. It doesn't matter whether you were just trying to release the balloon's true potential, or if you were extra nice to the balloon beforehand – it will still pop.

There are many ways to prompt people to better themselves, but 'If you don't do as well as my view of you dictates, I'll be really disappointed in you' isn't really the best. The subtext is 'Even though you did well this time, it might not be enough next time.'

- **Social status bribery** – *'You'll be a legend...'*

There's usually alcohol or false bravado involved in this case. This one's tricky, because it's so easy to fall for. You feel as if, far from just fitting in, you'll be actually appreciated if you just do this one dare, or down that one pint.

Step back. Unless you're somehow curing cancer or solving world hunger by virtue of whatever trivial act someone is goading you to do, you won't go down in history. Bards will not sing of your exploits, history books won't be adorned with pictures of you staring wistfully into the distance. There isn't a Nobel Prize for scaffold-climbing or pint-downing, as far as I know. (That said, if you're reading this and you're part of the Nobel committee, there's a niche there. I'm just saying.)

- **Adoration-based direction** – *'He/she will love you for it...'*

See above. Life isn't a perfume advert; the idea that the object of your affection will fall into your arms, or jump at the chance to be your friend over your readiness to succumb to peer pressure is a somewhat weak one. Besides, if they do, you have to wonder what their intentions were in the first place and why they find blind obedience so desirable.

- **Detrimental reassurance** – *'Go for it, we're all friends, you'll be fine...'*

'You'll be fine, we'll look after you.' This is a common scenario that often sees the person under pressure being persuaded to take something, whether it be recreational drugs, alcohol or something from a shop. This involves you entrusting your freedom, possibly even your life, to your friends. Things can, and do, go wrong, especially because when this situation occurs the people in question are usually under the influence themselves.

The crux of the matter is that in this situation people are telling you to do things and asking you to trust them completely. Figuratively, and often literally, they are asking you to put your life in their hands. Do you trust them implicitly? Would you trust them with your life? If the answer is no, don't do it. If the answer is yes, still don't do it – if you trust them completely, then chances are you care about them enough not to burden them with such a grave responsibility. Just say 'No thanks', and turn the conversation to something else.

- **Emotional blackmail** – *'So you don't care then? Do it for me.'*

This form of pressure is any kind of context that uses emotions to gain leverage in return for some kind of favour. Interestingly enough, the context I heard this in was from someone who used to be friends with a commission-based charity collector. The person used to make her feel callous for not signing up to a monthly donation scheme by inferring that she didn't care about their cause.

In the past, for me, this has been used by 'friends' who have cared more about having fellow casualties to share in their mistakes than friendship. As I grew older, I realised that misery loves company – I cut ties with people who, to influence me, would imply I didn't care, and I became happier for it. If you find yourself privy to this kind of pressure, you need to wonder whether this person, or these people, care about you – nobody has the right to manipulate another person like this.

- **Past-self pressurising** – *'You used to be awesome, the old you would have done it!'*

The past is often viewed through rose-tinted glasses, and often your past will come back to haunt you. It may manifest in strange ways though, and this kind of pressure is a great example of that. In this situation, your past self is painted in beautiful colours, brimming with confidence and spontaneity, and the pressure is on you to match up to this deified version of yourself.

There are so many subtexts to this that it almost falls under both spoken and unspoken categories of peer pressure. It feels as though the oppressor (I use this word in the most forgiving of lights, as it is as easy to find yourself applying peer pressure as it is to be affected by it) is almost implying that they were friends with the old you, and not the new you, that you've changed, that you're not fun to be around anymore. For added effect, this is often mixed with calls of, 'We never see you anymore!'

This reality, this past-self superhero envisioned by those who would influence you to do things you're reluctant to do, simply doesn't exist. In the past, everyone will have made as many negative decisions as they have positive ones, but as we grow older we learn from our mistakes. Life is one big trial and error experiment and, as the philosopher and poet George Santayana said, 'Those who cannot remember the past are condemned to repeat it.'

- **Playing to insecurities** – *'The only reason you won't do it is because you can't.'*

Our frail human psyche is riddled with insecurities – even some of the strongest minds are still plagued by doubt. To some extent this is a good thing; our inability to rest on our laurels leaves us constantly striving for personal betterment. Other times, it can be almost debilitating, feeling not just that we aren't good enough, but that we may never be good enough. It is in these times that we are at our most vulnerable, and often our most malleable.

It is at our most insecure times, at our darkest hours, that we often find ourselves making our most rash decisions. Very often, while searching for the acceptance of some, or the defiance of others, we succumb to external pressure and lose a little bit of ourselves in the moment.

From personal experience, apathy has been my best friend in this case. This kind of goading only works if you care about it, and the first step to not caring is pretending you don't. The root of the matter is that you have no obligation to prove yourself – be confident in who you are. Often flat-out refusal, with a sarcastic 'Yeah, sure', has seen this kind of situation through. This type of pressure is reactive – you rise to it, and then the people applying the pressure will react in turn. Break the chain; don't allow yourself to give too strong a reaction, and just decline.

- **Cut-off compulsion** – *'If you don't do it, you won't have anyone, or anything...'*

One of the important things to note about peer pressure is that you often find yourself applying it yourself, without any malice or ill-will in mind. I have frequently heard myself uttering the words, 'Go on, you know you want to', to that part of me that wants to stay in when I have already planned a games night. Stopping it from becoming detrimental stems from simply being self-aware and realising when you are doing it.

However, this form of pressure is one of the most deplorable and difficult to justify as a third party. It hardly qualifies as pressure, as it is almost a threat. Unfortunately, this is often the basis for a number of abusive friendships and relationships. It's often so difficult to get out of this situation; you feel worthless, as if you couldn't do better anyway and if you don't do what your oppressor is saying, you'll be left alone, and you'll have nothing. The kicker here is, there are always other people, you will always make other friends, but more than that, *you are simply better off alone.*

UNSPOKEN PEER PRESSURE

- **Learned behaviour** – *Pavlovian compulsion.*

Nothing to do with any type of raspberry dessert, this type of unspoken peer pressure is the reason a lot of people dress and act as they do. The term comes from the 'Pavlov's Dog' experiment showing classic conditioning, whereby a dog would come to associate a bell ringing with being fed. In the same vein, if we receive positive social stimuli when looking or acting a certain way, we will continue to repeat those conditions to receive the same favourable stimuli in the future. Of course, every rule has its exceptions, and often receiving criticism from others for a certain behaviour and/or dress can become almost a badge of honour, especially in certain fashion subcultures.

- **Media pressure** – *The golden carrot complex.*

Everybody, young or old, has fallen prey to this kind of pressure at some point in their life, consciously or otherwise. We are all constantly absorbing various types of advertising and we don't really get to choose whether we want to view them or not. Billboards, shop fronts, phone booths, television adverts – all come together to shape what we consume. Collectively, for example, the UK alone watched 2.7 billion TV ads in 2012, and averaged around four hours of television viewing per day, according to TV marketing research experts Thinkbox.

All of this viewing, along with carefully placed celebrity endorsement, conglomerates to form a kind of 'societal average' in terms of fashion and culture. This creates pressure on people to become culturally compliant with these norms. At best, someone who doesn't fit to these standards – exhibiting a different haircut, different dress sense and different film and media preferences – will be singled out as dissimilar and treated as such. (This is not always a bad thing! Sometimes, these differences are celebrated.) At worst, however, these abject differences can garner distrust, or dislike, and can lead to pressure to conform, often in the form of certain types of bullying.

- **Oppression prevention** – *Conformity based bully-proofing.*

This one is pretty easy to work out; it is very common, and very much tied into the last type of unspoken peer pressure. The difference, however, is that this is geared towards preventing bullying. This is a kind of 'bully-proofing', often the go-to for those who have been bullied themselves in the past. I've personally known countless people who have changed their style, what type of media they consume and even the way they speak to avoid oppression and bullying tactics from other people.

There are many different types of bullying, which will be elaborated on later in the book, but a lot of the time the idea is simply to avoid standing out as a potential target, nothing more. A person standing out from a crowd can be like a red rag to a bull in terms of would-be aggressors, especially since bullying can often stem from a distrust of something unusual or diverse.

This kind of pressure is self-perpetuating and insidious, potentially forcing someone into a life so mundane and self-expressionless that it is only slightly better than the alternative it is so carefully set out to prevent. This is certainly a type of pressure that parents would do well to watch out for, and is often characterised by frustration and apathy on return from school or college, which may not be evident during the day.

COPING WITH IT ALL

Stress is, unfortunately, all-pervasive. It weighs down on us and, if left unchecked, can grind us down until the cracks start to show. When this happens, there are two things that can happen – we vent, or in the case of someone with autism, it can lead to a meltdown. Even though stress affects us all, everyone has different tolerances and experiences different amounts of stress.

We have established, and re-established, that being a teenager is hard. It's no small wonder that teenage angst is so prevalent in the music scene – there seems to be no solace to be found from parents, teachers or even peers. If being a teenager is hard, being a teenager with Asperger's can be doubly so – so much of adolescent life relies on catching non-verbal cues and reacting accordingly that it can often feel as if the rest of the world developed psychic powers and you didn't get the memo.

As I've touched on briefly, people with autism tend to cope in different ways to other people, but whether stress is internalised or externalised, both ways of dealing with strain can take their toll. It is important to note that for someone on the autism spectrum, there are many more stressors faced throughout an average day than for someone without the disorder. As such, whether you have an ASD yourself, or you are working with or caring for someone with one, it's important to watch to make sure you *are* dealing with it. It's very easy to stick your head in the sand and pretend that whatever is causing the aggravation isn't happening, or just to melt down and lash out, but neither of these reactions helps in the long term.

Often, I hear the term 'exhibiting challenging behaviour' used to describe people who react externally to stressors. I have very mixed feelings about 'challenging behaviour', as it is a very open term and is often spoken of 'from the outside'. I haven't had friends with autism talk to me about their 'challenging behaviour', or indeed talk about any of their behaviours as challenging. I've heard talk of challenging situations and challenging people. I've had people calling me out when I have no idea I'm doing anything different to upset the status quo. I've had people call me odd, strange or weird, when I'm simply talking or just existing. *That* is challenging behaviour, in the most literal sense of the word. People challenging you for seemingly inconsequential actions is challenging, and that's tough to deal with. What's quite ironic is that this 'calling out of autism' often leads to so-called 'challenging behaviour'.

Challenging behaviour can become evident in the form of disruptive, often physically aggressive, behaviour. It can manifest in extreme forms, like self-harm, scratching, biting oneself or others, or through things like flapping or pica. What's important to note is that these are reactions to external stimuli, and when analysing how to deal with challenging behaviour, the cause is often overlooked. Helping to avoid or deal with the cause of challenging behaviour is much more important than dealing with the behaviour itself.

One thing which is grossly overlooked, on such a grand scale that I cannot even *begin* to stress this enough, is that challenging behaviour isn't always externally manifested. The person who flaps or bites or screams needs help when they get to that point, and help to avoid coming to that point, but keep an eye out for those who don't do these things. The quiet children who don't cause much hassle, but avoid physical contact, who quietly put their hands over their ears at levels of noise that seem innocuous, who seem distant during group activities – these children need help too. These are the ones who internalise everything, the ones without any form of vent or outlet, and often parents, teachers and carers don't realise there are problems until it's too late to remedy the core issues.

Whether someone on the autism spectrum internalises or externalises stress, at some stage a breaking point, or a meltdown, will be reached. Although a number of things can cause this, I can categorically say that sensory issues will be the root of the problem, since we perceive the world through touch, smell, sound, sight and taste. It may sound as if I'm being pedantic here – and spoiler alert, I am – but it's to prove a point. As I've already mentioned earlier, in the 'Sensory issues and autism' section in Chapter 1, everything is a product of sensory input, and when your senses are so tuned to outside stimuli, there are a number of things that can cause a person with an ASD to reach breaking point. It's important to work backwards from the original meltdown to find out exactly what caused it, and how it can possibly be avoided or (as will be the case for most things) simply dealt with better.

Obviously it's easy to sit here comfortably behind my laptop and write these things, but I write with the understanding of someone who has witnessed meltdowns, dealt with meltdowns and had meltdowns myself. At the time they can seem all-pervasive, all-encompassing, and the worst thing that could happen. The thing is, however, they *do* end, and afterwards things can seem clearer – and as I've stated previously, it's a sign that things have reached breaking point, and it can help point to things that need to be altered.

There are a number of things that can be done, and that often people with an ASD do autonomously, to keep things from reaching breaking point. However, sometimes the things that people do to alleviate stress can be detrimental to themselves or to other people. The person trying to cope may not even recognise that what they are doing is damaging, especially if what they are doing impairs their judgement somewhat. There are certain ways to deal with stress that are positive – cognitive behaviour therapy (CBT), meditation, counselling or even just taking some time out for themselves, to name but a few. However, the list of harmful activities is expansive too – self-medication, alcoholism, drug abuse and self-harm are some but by no means all the ways people find to keep their demons at bay.

Poor coping techniques or 'detrimental distractions' rarely just occur out of nowhere. Damaging handling techniques can be ones that are nurtured over time. In this sense, substance abuse, such as alcoholism, can manifest as a symptom rather than a standalone condition. When times get tough, a drink after a hard day can be a way to stave off the stress, and this can turn into a daily event. This can then lead to a couple or a few bottles of booze, first every evening, and then earlier and earlier, leading to daytime drinking. Before you know it, you have a whole problematic spiral of events that can be very difficult to escape from. People on the autism spectrum are generally very routine-bound anyway, and destructive routines become 'locked in' just as easily as positive ones.

Recognising when you aren't dealing with stress is key to getting 'on the right track' in terms of stress management strategies. It's like playing an experiential game of 'connect the dots'. Look at the times you are drinking or smoking or locking yourself away. Start to analyse the events that led up to this, and whether the act occurred soon after the event – it's easy to have the consequence overshadow the cause.

The cause-and-effect relationship between negative external stimuli and destructive coping mechanisms is a difficult one to break, but part of the secret to doing so lies in dissociating the cause and the consequence. If you manage to work out the cause of the destructive habit, you can do something positive afterwards to break the cycle. While as an intervention this sounds flimsy at best, humour me for a little while. To explain this in a little more detail, let's say you have a terrible day, or even just a tiring or stressful one. (NB: A lot of people with ASD have a much lower threshold for a 'stressful day'. There are few situations, whether in employment or day-to-day life, that involve no human interaction, and social interaction is hard for someone with autism. That's just the way it is, and through life it doesn't get any easier – you just get a little better at coping with it.) After a stressful day, a lot of people reach for the bottle, or something equally destructive. In moderation, this can be fine, but when substances are being used purely to blot something out, moderation doesn't come easy. So, we have the cause – the stressful day – and the effect – the destructive behaviour. Dissociating the two lies in driving a wedge between those two events, making it more difficult for the brain to draw psychological ties between them. If instead, or even to begin with, before you engage in destructive behavioural patterns you do something else (or if you're a parent or carer, you instigate something else, in which case be firm, but not aggressive) – whether it be going for a run, playing video games or undertaking something you're passionate about – you start to break the damaging routines that can seem almost gospel.

Now, talking about alcohol consumption or smoking, activities that aren't imminently lethal, is one thing but what about activities that are implicitly harmful no matter which way you look at it? There are some methods people use to cope that are unhealthy and dangerous. Self-harm, hard-drug abuse, suicidal ideation – there is no moderating these activities and often the border between them blurs somewhat. While I'm not going to fall into a debate on drug criminalisation, one thing any person can be sure about is that at least here in the UK, when you take an illegal drug, for recreational reasons or otherwise, you have no idea what's in it. There is no intermediary, no standard, no safeguard – a person must get lucky every time, and for that reason, at least in terms of coping mechanisms, I'm staunchly putting heavy drug use in the same category as self-harm.

There are a number of things that can help a person cope when circumstances become difficult, especially when you're near breaking point. There can be moments where destructive activities can seem like the only way out, or at least the only way to achieve a respite. It's difficult to cut through the fog at points like this; when everything seems so dark it can be hard to see any way out that doesn't involve simply blotting out memories for a little while. However, there are ways.

One thing I cannot stress enough is that if you punish yourself for feeling low, and for the inevitable lack of productivity that accompanies this, you won't be able to move forward. It's okay to struggle sometimes, it's simply part of life. A strange and somewhat unfortunate product of the 21st century is that often people's affinity with social media, and their subsequent 'digital lives', can give the illusion that everyone is happy and that any unhappiness is just a blip on the radar. There is nothing like a quick flick through the social media website of your choice to make you feel inadequate. The thing to remember is that it *is* an illusion – everyone has their trials and tribulations. Yes, some people deal with theirs better, but no one is exempt. The chances are that the high-flying rock-star-cum-skydiver inundating their online friends with pictures of their most recent idea to save the world with a spatula and a grain of rice probably stood in dog-shit at some point. Call me crass, but the crux of the argument lies intact nonetheless; making mistakes is an immensely human quality and we're all united in that fact.

In recent years, society as a whole has been guilty of mixing up biological ailments and afflictions of the human psyche on a grand scale. The brain has ceased to be viewed as a bodily organ and has been elevated to an almost out-of-body level. When it's viewed like this, however, it becomes easy to forget that when our general health suffers, so too does our mood. It makes sense that when our health is low, the body tries to avoid infection or damage by keeping us from wanting to do anything, and we feel tired, sluggish and fed up. This is known among psychologists as 'sickness behaviour', and especially when you think of it on an evolutionary scale, where a case of the flu could make the difference between being a predator's next meal or not, it makes a lot of sense.

When the notion of general health and psychological well-being is given due credence, the idea of exercise and a good diet as an 'upper' makes more sense. While these alone are in no way cures for depression – a subject for a later chapter – they do help. At least on a personal level, I found it difficult in the past to accept that exercise and diet play such a large role in terms of mood. I felt that to acknowledge this was to cheapen the emotions that play such a large part in our lives. Whether we like it or not (and I cannot stress enough that I'm not talking about depression and related disorders here – exercise and diet can help, but they are part of a much bigger interventional picture) our diet and how we look after our bodies play a bigger role in how we feel than we care to admit. In this sense, when it comes to being low and dealing poorly with stress, prevention is better than cure. At the risk of sounding (horribly) clichéd, look after your body, and to some extent your body will look after you. Regulating your sleep pattern, making sure you are eating properly and doing some exercise helps. You don't need to be Mo Farah to be eating and exercising properly – as a rule, if you're getting to bed before midnight and eating at least some vegetables and fruit, then you're doing okay.

Every so often, the best thing you can do is simply take some time for yourself to take your mind off things. This can be doing anything you enjoy. The chances are, if as a teenager or adult you have ever been at a low point in your life (and if you haven't, stop reading, put the book down, and mail in to let us all in on the secret), you have probably already been given this advice; this doesn't make it any less true. As we grow up, a lot of the things we do are not for ourselves but for other people, whether directly or indirectly. We study, putting undue pressure on ourselves, to make our parents proud. When we have children, we put our needs aside to better cater to theirs. This becomes such a part of our lives, it is almost an autonomous process, as natural as breathing. A side-effect of this 'auto-selflessness' is that, in the same way people aren't aware of their breathing 24 hours a day, people often don't realise that in doing this they can neglect their own self-worth. Look back – how much time have you taken recently to do something purely for yourself? If you had to think too long on that one, the chances are it isn't much.

'Taking time out for yourself' is a very vague notion, but it seems to be served well by its ambiguousness. Activities vary from person to person, and it's important to keep that in mind, especially when it comes to people on the autism spectrum. When times get really tough, some people write or play the guitar, others flap their arms, or I don't know, walk round in circles in the kitchen because it's the only thing that clears their mind. Fair enough, 'when the going gets tough, the tough walk round in circles' doesn't have quite the same ring to it, but the point is that one person's coping strategy, as long as it's not harming themselves or others, is just as viable as another person's. I'm sometimes approached by people who give this kind of behaviour the aforementioned label of 'challenging behaviour'. An interesting notion around this is the idea that walking in circles (during permissible times) or flapping is somehow 'challenging'. Challenging behaviour is not behaviour that makes you uncomfortable because you don't know its origins. It's not the person on the spectrum who is exhibiting challenging behaviour, it's the person calling out that behaviour for no good reason. It's the person *challenging* them.

I want to end this section by calling attention to a certain point; namely, the fact I have written a sub-chapter on coping, and made a large part of it focused on meltdown, or definitively *not* coping. The reason for this is that if you learn to cope with the darkest times, whether it's you dealing with it or a third party, you'll find the little struggles much easier. In this case, it's better to start from the bottom up. If you start by dealing with full-on cataclysm, then the anxiety, the struggles, seem less apocalyptic. At the end of the day, if you start from rock bottom, the only way to go is up.

MENTAL HEALTH AND AUTISM

Autism and mental health issues, unfortunately, tend to go hand in hand with each other. It can be conjectured that this is because people with some form of ASD are subject to so much more stress in general than people who aren't on the spectrum. Every situation takes constant memorising and recall of various types of social ethos, social faux pas are so much more regular and debilitating, and personal relationships are steeped in complex issues regarding the mind and the heart. Of course, there are good points (and some born directly of the bad – in dealing with these issues, one can certainly develop a particularly thick skin), but these are issues that can cause stress which can mount up over time and either lead to endogenous mental health issues, or exacerbate or activate underlying ones brought forth by genetic or personal disposition.

Having an autism spectrum disorder and dealing with mental health issues at the same time is both tough and somewhat experientially cacophonous. Years ago, I started to exhibit some behaviours not particularly relevant to autism. I'd have weeks where I wanted to be out all the time and constantly wanted to be around people. I wanted to be the centre of every party, and everything was great. If I had any problems – money, relationship issues and family issues – they were easily solvable. I could sort them somehow, and at the time they weren't important. I was invincible, I could do anything and I intended to do everything; I'd make up the wildest of plans, plans that had no chance of ever being brought to fruition. This sounds great, but what goes up must come down.

What would follow was an immense crash of dizzying proportions. How it always happened was so simple I could almost trace it. There would be one negative thought and just like that it would branch off into two more, then two more after that, and my mood would simply spiral downwards. It was inexorable and at the time it felt as if there was little to nothing I could do about it. I didn't want to talk to anyone and being around people was impossible. Every word had to be dragged out of me, I couldn't think straight, and I just wanted to do anything to distract myself that didn't involve socialising in any sense. It wasn't just that I felt incredibly worthless, but alongside that I felt selfish and stupid for thinking like that. I was broken, defunct, a shell of what I was, and the juxtaposition to a mere week or two before was stark, and seemingly impossible. I'd had mood swings before, but this was something different, and it was entirely dark. My room was my solace and I'd just sit and play games, read or just sleep for weeks on end.

The lows were the worst and I seemed to spend more time down than I did up. This was compounded by the fact that I was constantly reaping the 'benefits' of the times when I was up. I'd go out all the time, take random train journeys to random places, and then end up high and dry. I'd wind up completely broke and depressed, and it was a grim cycle to be a part of. Eventually, things went from bad to worse, and after about a week or two of highs, I ended up crashing in a big way. After being alone for around a week or two, I said I was heading out into town. To cut a long story short, I ended up standing at the top of a car park meaning to jump. I got pulled down and was put in a psychiatric ward, leading to three of the strangest, most surreal months of my entire life.

My moods, which had previously been like a low-rate rollercoaster ride, went crazy. I went from the most crushing lows to the most ridiculous manic episodes. I'm in no way stupid, the severity was very definitely endogenous, but it was a reaction to the situation I was in. I went from having my freedom to being locked up in a ward where all we had were a few 15-minute breaks every day to go out for a cigarette. I slept in a bed on a ward with eight other people and some of the things I saw during those times will haunt me for the rest of my life, things I have told nobody about since. While this was a grim time for me, the one thing it did was push me to get better. I vowed never to get to that point again.

Looking back, it was quite obvious that I was showing presentations of bipolar disorder, but it took me a long time to actually get diagnosed. Part of this was nonsensical; I was repeatedly told that mood swings were just a part of the diagnostic canon for Asperger's Syndrome, once from a doctor who suggested a blood test to check for the levels of Asperger's in my blood. Other times the highs were just taken as me recovering from depressive episodes. It was only when I organised all the other service users to run a marathon around the ward at 4am that the idea was taken seriously. There followed a long time where I kept a daily mood diary, with a 1–10 mood-rating system, and had weekly meetings with a psychiatrist. We put the ratings together in a graph and saw a very prominent pattern in terms of mood. It was good to see; when things are quantified and put together in a way you can see clearly, you can start to make a little more sense of them, and find ways to work on them. In this sense, even though I didn't feel as if I needed a diagnosis, it was a relief for me when I was diagnosed.

Bipolar disorder and Asperger's Syndrome, in particular, can be very contrary to each other. When I'm low, I want to keep away from people and conversations are forced and tepid. Stringing words and sentences together vocally is incredibly hard work and I really have to push myself to form the most basic of conversations. However, when I'm on a high I want to socialise. I want to be around people, to talk, to challenge myself. I'm well aware of the social hangovers, the stress and anxiety caused by 'running an emulator' for too long, but the nature of the high means I just don't care about that. Everything is tomorrow's problem, and today is the now.

Depression is a crushing yet entirely mundane beast. It brings forth great contradictions; having suicidal ideations while in fits of laughter, being completely hopeless while in the midst of promising life changes, or feeling entirely alone in the heart of a crowd. It isn't a climactic fall into oblivion, but a slow and inexorable spiral, like water swirling down the drain. It is a very real illness that, if left unchecked and unaided, can kill. The behavioural links between depression and autism and Asperger's Syndrome have not been the subject of much research in recent years, with most studies dating back to the late 1990s. There are a number of possible reasons for this, but most probable is the difference in presentation between people with depression alone and people with depression as a comorbidity with ASD. Whereas people with depression will become disinterested in things they enjoy as they don't derive the same pleasure from them, someone with Asperger's Syndrome, for example, will throw themselves into their specialist subject, often obsessing over it to the point that they forego things like hygiene, food and sleep. When asked, as part of the standardised Goldberg depression test, whether they've lost interest in things they enjoy, their answer is going to be no. Different presentations like this make it a little more difficult to diagnose depression as an autism comorbidity.

Counteracting the symptoms of depression will never be a walk in the park, but it is possible. A lot of depressive episodes can start because of certain ways of thinking. It can start with one thought, which can lead to another, and another, and another. Before long, it can lead to a full episode, causing insomnia, agoraphobia, lack of concentration, and suicidal ideation. Depression can be manageable; there is this myth that's been propagated in recent years that people with depression are never happy, that they are somehow tedious or self-absorbed. In reality, often people with depression are more generous than some, not self-absorbed. They laugh louder and find joy in everyday situations more easily. When you've hit the lowest of the low, the good times seem brighter by contrast. Often people with depression can be outgoing and lively. Changing the triggers that lead to a depressive episode is difficult, but there are certain ways of doing so.

- **Push yourself to go outside:** Even when you feel like staying in, pushing yourself to go outside is a good idea. Both the sun and fresh air do help, and making yourself socialise is important even when you don't feel like it. When it comes to Asperger's in particular, being sociable is something that needs to be practised. When you spend extended periods of time alone, social skills, which are already difficult, get rusty, and this breeds anxiety. One of the reasons people on the autism spectrum are under so much pressure is the possibility that they will make a social faux pas; this breeds the type of anxiety that leads to depressive episodes. When you're terrified that everything you do might be in some way wrong, you're too scared to even go outside.

  If you've ever heard of the popular saying, 'Do one thing every day that scares you', be aware that for someone on the autism spectrum this is true for most days. For someone on the spectrum with depression, this can be every day. There were so many times that I was chastised for not doing something, or leaving things out, or seeming lazy. I always felt like screaming back, 'I'm up, and I'm out of my room. Isn't this enough? Do you know how hard this is?' Never underestimate a person with depression who is out and about, a person laughing and chatting. That person isn't cured or faking it – that person has looked their struggles in the face and smiled.

- **Exercise helps:** Granted, when you're feeling the lowest of the low, going out for a run is likely to be near the bottom of your to-do list (supposing you have one, of course). However, a little bit of exercise genuinely helps during depressive episodes by releasing endorphins and providing a booster to mood. Reviews of current research mostly conclude that while exercise is better than no intervention, it's not a viable treatment path by itself. Sometimes the achievement you feel by pushing yourself to go and exercise helps in and of itself, though.

Exercise worked for me, to a point, but I'd definitely recommend it as part of the 'bigger picture' as opposed to a simple standalone treatment method. The reason exercise worked for me was because I'd make short-term goals, like a five- or ten-kilometre run, or a certain route, and then train for that. That way I was able to work up to a target rather than just exercising for the sake of it. Some people find it easier to just exercise 'on the fly', so to speak, but others find it better to work up to something.

- **Cut down specialist subject engagement**: When someone is depressed, interest in subjects and activities they usually enjoy tends to wane or disappear completely. However, someone with Asperger's Syndrome or autism and depression will tend to immerse themselves in their specialist subject. From an outside point of view, this can detract from a diagnosis; the person appears to be gaining enjoyment from the activity, and therefore is exhibiting symptoms differing from the base criteria for depression. However, during depressive episodes the specialist subject often goes from a cause of enjoyment to a compulsion, something that *needs* to be done. It becomes the only thing that the person finds control in during times where control is lacking. The activity ceases to become something pleasurable. It becomes the last bastion in a world being broken down, and its lack of completion feels almost tantamount to defeat or annihilation.

When it gets to this point, it's important to be careful how you go about regaining that activity as a recreation rather than a compulsion. If you simply cut the specialist interest right down, you risk causing a meltdown. There are a number of things to think about here: when you cut down something that somebody has been filling entire days with to one or two hours straight off, you bring two issues to the fore. First, that last bastion of control I spoke about? That's now stripped away. And second, what do you do in the time usually allotted to that subject? When I cut down or had restrictions placed on time engaging in a specialist subject, it was often replaced with time spent ruminating, worrying about things that could go wrong. I spent whole days in a panic as I felt my life gradually slipping out of control.

Rome wasn't built in a day – don't rush when it comes to replacing time spent engaging with a special interest. Find other things to do instead and be constructive in what you choose. Often when you're depressed, day-to-day things like washing your clothes, showering, and chores become lost. It sounds mundane (and it is) but try to regain those activities, bit by bit. There's a sense of achievement to be found in doing the 'normal' things, and it makes you feel a little more human, at least for a while. There's no rush, and don't expect to go straight to doing regular day-to-day things all at once – just take things a day at a time. Obviously, you can't fill every bit of time outside your specialist subject with banal tasks, which leads me onto my next point.

- **Self-reflection, little and often:** This is an important one; it can be very easy, when everything and everyone seems to be against you, to lash out at those you care about when they're trying to help. However, it's even easier to miss that you're doing so. Make sure to reflect little, but often on how you affect other people. Even though depression can make a person introverted, often their actions can affect other people negatively.

- **Get passionate about something else:** If you have a specialist subject, find something you enjoy outside of that and invest some of your time in it. Start a project, big or small, but keep the goals short term – that's the key. The nature of depression is that you don't know what the next day is going to hold, whether you're going to get a break or be in the depths of despair. If you start adding long-term goals to this, then you're not only going to add stressors, but you'll make yourself feel like a failure if you don't match up to these self-imposed deadlines. Stick to daily goals, then weekly if you feel as if you can deal with that. Just don't make things unrealistic; when you set yourself up for failure, you only drive yourself deeper into depression.

Lower your expectations when it comes to dealing with depressive episodes. When simply getting out of bed is a struggle, you should be looking at maybe taking up a new hobby rather than organising a skydiving excursion. If you do find that you fail in your self-allotted task, don't be dissuaded – there is always tomorrow. Anxiety about whether or not you'll finish something that you yourself have elected to do is completely counterproductive.

- **Don't suffer in silence**: When it comes to theory of mind or 'putting yourself into someone else's shoes', people on the autism spectrum don't do so well. For me this extends beyond forgetting that other people's feelings and beliefs are different to my own, and all the way to forgetting that people's thoughts are different to my own. This means I often forget that people don't know what I'm thinking. This extends towards many people with ASD, and it can be problematic in terms of depression.

  Something completely contrary to the theory of mind issues for those on the autism spectrum (particularly the idea that if you think and feel a certain way, so will others) is the feeling that when you are depressed, you are completely alone. A great many people have suffered from depression at some point in their life, whether homogenous (clinical) or endogenous (environmentally induced). If you are going through a depressive episode, take comfort in the fact that a lot of people will have been through some form of what you're experiencing. Tell someone what you're going through, in whatever way you can. Paint it, draw it, design it, write it, photograph it – find a medium where you are a little more comfortable disclosing 'big subjects' – and tell someone. If speaking to someone you know is difficult, speak to someone objective. Even though there will be waiting lists in terms of counselling, it's worth speaking to someone.

Mental health issues are exactly that – they are issues but they can be dealt with. They cause difficulties, but these are difficulties that can be managed. People with depression can be happy, and people with bipolar can be euthymic, or level. At times these issues can be impairing, at other times debilitating. However, they are not, as some of the recent publicity mental health issues has garnered would suggest, inherently dangerous, nor do they mean that people can't lead normal and healthy lives. There is so much stigma attached to mental illness, which is bizarre when you consider that one in four people in the UK will be diagnosed with some form of mental illness at some point in their lives. These are still very misunderstood conditions and there needs to be a lot more awareness around the subject.

3
WORK AND EDUCATION

EARLY EDUCATION, FOR ME, was not an easy time and I'm fairly sure a lot of people on the autism spectrum who went through high school had a similarly rough experience. I'm not going to focus on school life throughout, as I covered school life pretty extensively in *Freaks, Geeks and Asperger Syndrome*. (Yes, that was a shameless plug.) What I am going to cover, however, is dealing with the fallout from a negative schooling experience. If you had a great school life, then that's wonderful. If you didn't, however, and if the experience was negative, it can leave lasting scars that can be detrimental to not just your future education, but your life from then on. By 'negative experience' I don't just mean that there were days when you were bored, or you didn't have fun, or you didn't feel like going in. I mean if there were days when the thought of getting up and going to school made you physically ill, where sometimes the anxiety got so bad that even the idea of it was enough to send you into a panic.

If the last sentence of the last paragraph resonated with you, then you have my commiserations – school wasn't a good time for you either. I went through a number of schools trying to find a formula that worked for me, and ended up being home schooled after everything culminated in my taking an overdose and ending up in a coma. Every aspect of school was difficult for me and I couldn't find a way to make it work. The sounds were too loud and unexpected to cope with; every school bell was another shock to the system. The lights flickered and each day was a new headache. People there were less than understanding, and detention became a welcome respite from the schoolyard. It became a common side-effect of the fights I got into for being 'weird', my mere existence apparently a blight to certain people.

No person should be subject to constant psychological and physical duress on a daily basis – such an existence has no place in the civilised world. School life shouldn't be any different. I said I wasn't going to dwell on the subject of school, but if you're reading this and you're still in school, and this sounds like your school life, you need to tell someone, in any way you can. Talking about feelings was never easy for me; I find it easier to write them down – if this is easier for you, then you should do it. The present is not worth jeopardising the future for.

Emotions and habits attached to caustic situations and experiences don't just disappear as soon as those events finish, and this is very important to consider when dealing with the fallout from negative experiences post-school. For a very long time after I finished school, I was plagued by agoraphobia and anxiety, and a deep distrust in humanity. Throwing off that weight was a long process; some of the ways I dealt with it helped, some hindered. While I didn't undergo it myself, I've heard from a lot of people that CBT helps deal with some of the anxiety, and talking through with family members helped me a great deal. Part of getting better, and reclaiming some sense of normality after any detrimental experience, is finding your best route to recovery. Each person is different and it's important to find what works best for you; your past and people close to you are the best ways to work this out. For me, gradual desensitisation worked best, challenging myself by putting myself into social situations to push me out of my comfort zone. There were too many times I pushed myself too far and ended up having a meltdown or a panic attack, and too many times when I didn't have an 'escape' when things got too much. If you want to challenge yourself and go down this route, then contingency planning is important - things can go wrong, situations can become too stressful and it's important to have an 'escape route' if they do.

While school itself can be difficult, so too can be time without it. A lack of structure can be problematic. It's important that you have something to do sometimes, as days where you have nothing to keep you company other than your own thoughts can be the worst. For me, the holidays were almost worse than school itself; all the anxiety that I'd harboured all through term time didn't just disappear as soon as the holidays began, and though the holidays heralded a reprieve from school life, they also meant days where there was no structure, nothing to distract me from my inner demons. I'm sure a lot of people reading this will agree that the mind can be a dark place and sometimes we are our own worst enemies.

Filling the days with something is important, whatever that is. If you get used to setting up a timetable early on, you'll find it much easier in later life. Lacking structure can leave you feeling lost and helpless, and often you find yourself filling the days with things that are less than constructive. Rudyard Kipling was right when he wrote in his poem 'If' that the common minute can be unforgiving and it can be hard to fill it with 'sixty seconds' worth of distance run'. We live in a world of distractions, both technological and otherwise, and it can be all too easy just to let time slip away. This isn't to say that you shouldn't have days where you let time just slip away – not at all. Often we need these 'defrag days' to get our thoughts in order. In the process of academic writing, this is called 'incubation' – leaving time to think and organise your thought process into something coherent so you can put down your thoughts properly.

FURTHER/HIGHER EDUCATION

We begin our journey into education with school. School is a strange place, full of unfamiliar faces and noises – we can learn some of them, but to learn them all broaches the realms of the impossible. It can be a difficult place for someone growing up with an autism spectrum disorder, and, by extension, for their siblings, parents and carers. Life in both further and higher education, however, is a strange place. In school we are taught facts and figures, and to some extent right from wrong. We are taught things which we assume to be right and we eschew that which isn't. After this, we graduate from secondary school and end up running into this big flashing neon sign that says, 'It's not quite as simple as that.' (It's not a literal sign by the way, just a metaphor. It still proves my point perfectly though, because even language is complex.) The first time I learned that some of my high school textbooks were wrong or outdated, it blew my mind. When we are young teenagers in secondary school, our teachers' words are gospel, so to find that we may have learned *wrong* information in school is just bizarre.

Obviously, while a portion of the information we take in is subjective, this is not to say that your secondary school teachers were, or are, just spouting opinion. It's very easy to say that everything is subjective, but, for example, whether you believe in gravity or not, you're not going to float away any time soon. Part of the beauty of humanity's ability to learn, however, is its ability to change perspective based on what's observed. When I was in school, we were taught that there are nine planets in the solar system we currently inhabit. Then, we discovered a planetary mass slightly larger than Pluto and the decision had to be made whether to have ten planets, maybe more, or to wipe Pluto's credentials as a planet. I digress, but by this I mean we observe, learn and then adjust our views depending on what we discover.

Further and higher education is an amazing thing that way – we don't just learn, we learn to *teach ourselves*.

The difference between further and higher education, at least in the UK, is denoted as the difference between college courses such as BTEC national diplomas and A-levels, and undergraduate study courses such as bachelor's degrees. The main difference between the two is that undergraduate and postgraduate courses in higher education are based around autonomous or 'self-led' study. This is the idea that other than targeted, open lectures, you source a lot of the supporting evidence for the work you do yourself. It's a very different form of studying, and it takes a lot of adjusting to, but it's massively liberating. Part of working autonomously involves managing your time and using it productively. Whereas in school you have timetabled lessons pretty much 9am–4pm weekly, when it comes to university, and to some degree, college, it's up to you to make sure you're hitting your deadlines and meeting your targets.

A lot of people with ASD and dyspraxia struggle with timekeeping and it's still something that I have problems with myself. However, with the accessibility of both free and paid timekeeping software, it is becoming easier to manage. One of the greatest mistakes I and a lot of other people make is not factoring in recreational time, and 'burning out'. One of the toughest parts of keeping a timetable, aside from this, is that life is non-linear. If you have a busy life in general you'll find that your timetable seems to reshuffle itself of its own accord a lot of the time. People will always make demands on your time, but reshuffling timetables when you have Asperger's can be difficult. A timetable fast becomes a routine, and when you change parts of it to factor in events such as chores and family responsibilities, which can often pop up out of the blue, it can be a shock to the system.

Very often, the trick to effective timetabling can be avoiding timetable-based routines altogether by setting targets instead of set time periods for work deadlines. For me, both writing this book and studying for a degree set new challenges in terms of time constraints and I was finding I'd spend more time reshuffling my timetable than I did working. More than this, I was suffering the same side-effects as I do when I break a 'set-in-stone' routine; I was feeling misplaced and disoriented and I'd find it immensely difficult to concentrate on anything. When I'd purposely put this time aside to work, this was a complete deal breaker. It meant that during time completely devoted to a specific task, I felt so unsettled that I couldn't focus on that task at all. To combat this, I've found that rather than setting time slots in terms of work or revision, i.e. working from 3pm to 5pm, making fluid targets works better. For example, when I started writing this book, I set targets to work from 10am to 5pm with an hour break. I found that whenever anything encroached on this time I couldn't concentrate and it became more and more difficult to reshuffle time efficiently. Now I have a daily target of 500 words a day; it's simple and achievable, but more to the point, it's not set in stone temporally. As long as I reach that target at some point in the day, I'm on schedule. The same can apply to coursework or reading; the target could be to read a certain number of pages or to complete a certain essay question. Part of the beauty of this way of working is that it can work within an existing timetable. In this sense, timetabled work hours become more fluid, and the hours themselves aren't the be all and end all, they are simply avenues to reach projected targets.

Recreational time can be a bit of a paradigm when it comes to timekeeping. First off, there are no half measures. On the one hand, it's important when creating a timetable to factor in time for 'defragging' and recreation – make it very clear that this time is books away, no-more-work chill time (unless reading is how you prefer to relax, in which case, don't put the book away). The other option is to leave it out completely. By this I don't mean just timetable work into every waking hour until your fingers bleed and you end up speaking primarily in Shakespearean prose or algebraic formulae. The idea of 'recreation by omission' is simply that you complete a certain target in a day and then the rest of the time is time spent on your own terms. I prefer this method as I am very aware of how quickly my mind likes to drop into routines, and so I try to make days as random as I can.

College and university tend to be a lot more accommodating than the primary and secondary schooling system, where the ethos of support tends to lack communication, is somewhat rigid and inflexible and is, frankly, a little autistic. When it came to university, I found that the support network was not only great, but also gave as much or as little support as I wanted. Something I learned the hard way, however, is that while the support is there, you need to ask for it! This sounds the most obvious thing in the world, but while I disclosed that I had an ASD, that I was dyspraxic and that I had bipolar disorder, I didn't disclose that I needed help, and exactly what kind of help I needed. While there are systems put into place to prevent this kind of thing from happening, it's all too easy to forget that other people don't know what you struggle with, especially when it comes to 'invisible disabilities'. I get told a lot of the time that you wouldn't know I had an ASD at first, and this is great, but looking as if you don't need help can be a barrier to getting support.

The important thing to remember in terms of support is that *you* decide the level of support you want. Going through college, I had a special educational needs coordinator (SENCO) with me in all lessons, and while the reminder of where I was supposed to be going was great, in lessons I found their presence distracting, and it was affecting my work. We spoke about it and agreed this wasn't needed in class, and so I just got the reminders. On top of this, I was able to use a laptop instead of pen and paper, as I write extremely slowly. I suppose the crux of the matter is that while it can sometimes be difficult to 'upgrade' in terms of support by gaining more than you currently have, establishments will rarely argue if a change of support means a decrease in resources needed to fund it. Just be very careful when making decisions to remove certain provisions, as getting them back if you decide you made a wrong decision can be problematic!

However well put together a support system may be, problems can and do crop up. Dealing with these promptly is key to moving forward, especially if they stymie your ability to work properly. I have, like many others, been in the situation where an issue I've been having has caused me to get behind on my work because I've waited to see if the situation would resolve itself. If you have a problem, don't just wait it out and see if it gets better! There are very few situations in life where this strategy works. Make sure you tell someone if there is something going wrong, both academically and in terms of welfare during college or university hours. Many people find it tough to articulate their problems, and many more people suffer from *l'esprit de l'escalier,* or 'the wit of the staircase' – thinking of the perfect thing to say long after the time to say it has passed. If this is you, you may find writing key words down before a support meeting helps, or even skipping the speech altogether and corresponding by email. I always find it much easier to articulate my thoughts in writing rather than speaking on a one-to-one basis; when dealing with your problems, as in many areas of life, you should always play to your strengths.

EMPLOYMENT

Education is at least linear in a certain way, and has a definitive beginning and end, but work is a different thing altogether. Work is a strange, often disorienting thing – it's a huge change from education, as a job carries a lot of responsibility. Unless you decide to work freelance in your chosen field of work (and even if you do, you may find that this still applies to you on occasion), there's a good chance you'll be working as part of a team. Working as a member of a team can include a number of things that people on the autism spectrum can find problematic; social interaction, face-to-face contact and communication of ideas are things I have always struggled with in a group setting. Unemployment in autism is rife, but there are a lot of successful people with ASD who lead healthy, and often wealthy, working lives.

Messing up in a job won't earn you a detention, but you may very quickly find yourself looking for a new position. It's vital you take responsibility for your actions by giving yourself the best head start you can, and this includes fully disclosing if you have an autism spectrum disorder when you apply. It doesn't affect your chances of getting a job and it isn't going to single you out as different within the workplace. Communication problems can arise in a multitude of different ways, from sensory difficulties to problems processing information quickly enough. The common denominator between high school, college, university and employment is that there is help available. It can be in different ways and can often be more difficult to obtain from one place than another, but it's still there. While obviously funding is always going to be an issue, often the help is rooted simply in people who are willing to understand, or even willing to just try to understand.

There are all kinds of jobs, but there is hardly a catalogue you can flick through to find which one is right for you. There will be certain vocations that you won't even have heard of, and others people will try to turn you away from. The problems that being on the autism spectrum can pose in the world of employment can seem all-pervasive. A large number of jobs, especially at entry level, involve face-to-face social interaction, rebranded as 'customer services'. When working full time, this can be absolutely exhausting – 'running an emulator', or 'pretending to be normal', for any length of time takes its toll, so doing this for 30 or 40 hours a week can be too much for someone with an ASD to handle.

Disclosure in the workplace is hugely important – it's so easy to just assume everything will be okay, especially when everything seems fine at the start. You've just started a new job, you feel great, empowered even. The kicker is that when something goes wrong, you're 'up shit creek without a paddle', as the old saying goes. If you seek support in the workplace, it doesn't make you in any way different, and it doesn't make you weak. Disclosure is an issue I've struggled with all through life, and it's stretched to employment, too – I never wanted to be construed as weak-willed in any way. The point is, however, that disclosing an ASD to an employer at your workplace doesn't change anything, and it's important to remember this. If you have an ASD, it doesn't matter whether you tell someone or not, you still have it, but if you let a prospective employer know, you have a safety net. If you have problems in the workplace attributed to being on the autism spectrum, then you can get the help you need before things spiral out of control.

Being in employment often means working as a member of a team and this can be problematic, but there are ways to combat the social anxiety that is often so intrinsically linked with situations such as this. Very often, people on the autism spectrum can fixate on a certain subject or set of subjects. This subject can be anything at all, and can reach the point of obsession, encroaching on day-to-day life to the point where it can be debilitating. However, sometimes this 'specialist subject' is allowed to flourish and can grow into something beautiful, and every so often will become the person's vocation. There is a certain media stereotype which seems to be propagated in recent years, of the 'stoic autistic' as a non-gesticulatory, iron-faced robot. This is completely untrue and nowhere is this more apparent than when a person on the spectrum is asked to talk about their passion, their specialist subject. In this sense, people with ASD can sometimes make the best team leaders. It's rare, but I've been in the situation before where a passion of mine has driven other people to do better in a related area, and it can be a great feeling. (I've also been in the situation where my passion for a subject has driven other people up the wall, which, while erring on the side of sadism, is a feeling I've definitely grown fond of as I grow older.)

Employment is going to entail a certain amount of social contact, and knowing how to conduct yourself in a work setting is important. In the world of employment there's a chance you'll find yourself making a great deal of acquaintances – the whole friendship/working relationship is an interesting one, full of idiosyncrasies. Knowing the difference between a friendship and a working relationship is crucial, and it is tough to keep a clear line between the two. A 'professional' relationship is the working relationship between colleagues, and is a vague subject to define – it's kind of halfway between a friend and an acquaintance. Some colleagues you will find you're closer to than other people, but at the very least in work time, your colleagues are your colleagues. I'm going to say conversation should be kept work based, because everyone knows one colleague where any conversation based on the big wide outside world is met with silence, steely eyes and a glassy smile that says in no unclear terms, 'Get back to work.' After asking around, and spending a lot of time thinking, I believe when it comes to work relationships the key word is neutrality.

Keeping neutrality in the workplace means keeping conversation light and knowing when certain conversational topics are 'out of bounds'. Humanity is a mixing pot of differing opinions, and this is a great thing. However, if you have very strong opinions on a topic, there's a pretty good chance that topic is not for use in conversation with customers or colleagues. This applies especially in a customer service environment. This can include (but isn't limited to):

- **Political stance:** Political leanings are an awful topic for the workplace. The trouble with politics is that whether you like it or not, declaring political allegiance will cause people to judge you one way or another. Whether you're left wing, right wing or firmly in the centre politically, politics is one bird that should be left outside your place of employment completely.

- **Medical issues:** While I've already said that it's worth being open with your employer about having an ASD, there are some things which you just shouldn't talk about in the workplace, and physical medical issues are definitely one of these. Nobody wants to hear about what you used to treat a nasty boil you had or about that trick knee of yours. When it comes to ASD and mental health, it's better to err on the side of caution. Who to tell and when is completely your choice, but I've found that some people who don't have prior knowledge in this matter can treat me differently afterwards, which can be, frankly, infuriating and has affected work performance in the past.

- **Religion:** Religion is a touchy subject in day-to-day life, never mind the workplace. There are people who are indifferent and people who harbour strong views on it, but it's often difficult to tell the difference and light conversations on people's opinions can often turn into a whole Pandora's Box of conflicting ideas. Steer clear of this one when it comes to colleagues.

- **Sex life:** Whether you see yourself as a bit of a Casanova, or whether you're going through a dry spell (which, by the way, is possibly one of the most wonderfully euphemistic metaphors I've ever heard when it comes to sex), this is just not workplace fodder. People tend to gossip, and some people can make snap decisions, leading to premature judgements.

- **Finances:** As with the previous point, there are certain personal issues that should very definitely be kept personal to avoid people making snap character judgements. To someone new, you complaining about monetary issues may come across as pestering for a loan or charity.

Alternatively, if you've just had a windfall, or things are going particularly well, that can appear as gloating or boastful, and this really isn't how you want to come across to new colleagues.

- **Social networking:** This is included as a 'blanket point' because in recent years this has become such a technological faux pas that it can be a complete deal breaker, and can potentially lose you your job. The biggest point here is that whether your social profile is set to private or not, you should never talk about your job, and never, ever, ever negatively. After a busy work day you may be tired, and social media can seem like a way to vent, but there is always the chance that any comment you put on could be relayed to your supervisor, or someone higher up. It's simply not worth it.

- **Work-based gossip:** Gossip is insidious – half-truths and hearsay living under the guise of fact. It is a game of Chinese whispers where everyone loses. Simply put, don't do it. The point is (and also possibly the biggest distinction between a friendship and a work-based relationship) that whatever you think about someone, even if the very sight of someone makes your blood boil, you can still maintain a proper working relationship. You don't have to like someone to work with them. However, once gossip starts flying around and it emerges that so-and-so doesn't like so-and-so, or John Doe said this about Joe Bloggs, you may find that civility takes its leave pretty quickly.

One of the biggest things to remember when it comes to employment and autism is that there are non-traditional routes to employment. I know I've put particular emphasis on playing to your strengths, but in both everyday life and autism this is a great way to be good at and to enjoy what you do. When I was younger I used to fret constantly that I'd never find a job in retail, never be able to work in a bar and might never be employed in customer services. It was only when people started to ask me whether I was selling my services as a photographer, and when I started to write earnestly, that I realised that thinking laterally can have its pros. Never be afraid to go for non-traditional routes of employment and, more importantly, if you're good at something, don't be afraid to let people know. The line between confidence and arrogance is a fine one and is easily crossed, but if you're good at something, more often than not work will find you.

4
BULLYING

BULLYING IS A STRANGE thing and is rooted in a number of issues. On researching for this chapter, I was in two minds whether to add it at all, as this book is based around issues faced in adulthood. The more research I did and the more people I asked, the more I realised that this is not only relevant but absolutely needed. It doesn't matter how old or young you are, people can be bullied at any age. Often, people don't realise it's happening until someone points it out. As physical bullying is far less tolerated in adulthood, bullying tends to take on more sinister forms, aimed at degrading a person. Bullying in adulthood is a form of control; it involves eroding a person's sense of self-worth until they feel completely powerless. The longer this kind of bullying goes on, the less likely someone is to retaliate.

The thing about bullying is that it's very often rooted in a fear of the different or unknown, which can make people with an ASD prime targets. People tend to distrust what they don't understand, and this is why the biggest threat and preventative measure to the somewhat insipid culture of bullying is knowledge. Bullying dies when empathy is employed; the more people gain knowledge of exactly how their actions affect other people, the less inclined they are to carry out those actions in future. The 'different' or 'unknown' encompasses a wide variety of subjects; people are bullied for their opinions, their mannerisms, their social class or their religion – and this list is far from exhaustive.

Fear is a terrible driving force. It makes people act in ways that often they wouldn't otherwise act. Through my own first-hand experience and from third-party experience, I've seen bullies who have used it as their entire modus operandi. While some people unfortunately just bully to make themselves feel bigger, others lack control in their own lives so completely that they feel they have to take it from other people. It's difficult to look past the actions of the stereotypical bully, that mean-spirited person who pushed you over at school or took every opportunity possible to belittle you in the workplace or used you in any way wherever and whenever possible. However, these actions can often simply be an attempt to keep some kind of grip, to claw back some degree of control from the ever-crumbling facade of their life.

Even after bullying has stopped, even long after, the person being bullied can be left empty, lacking the confidence they once had. It's a difficult topic to write about; I was bullied throughout my childhood and through some of my adult life, so I've had enough experience of it to know what it's like. Yet, it's not so far consigned to my past that I've forgotten about it or even, if I'm honest, forgiven some of the people involved. I always felt different – not unique, but like a round peg in a square hole – and all the while I was made to feel as if it was my fault. Bullying is cowardice – it's pushing a person to breaking point while making them accountable, but all the time never quite wanting them to get there. If something happens and the person being bullied is metaphorically or physically 'broken', and if they end up coming to harm, through accident, suicide, self-harm or any other means, the bullies will almost always show remorse, be it through legitimate empathy, the philosophy of 'we never meant it to go so far', or simply through fear of reprisal.

The road to regaining the confidence you shed after being bullied is a long and winding one. It takes a lot of things, but time and the patience needed to let that period pass are probably foremost in terms of importance. It can seem at the darkest times that nothing will ever be right, and it is then, when the nights are longest and the proverbial demons are at their loudest, that it's so important to keep in mind that *this, too, shall pass*. It doesn't happen overnight and it doesn't happen by itself, but give it time and it will happen. An equally huge part of the process of regaining your humanity, in terms of bullying, is acceptance. I don't mean simply accepting your fate, or accepting that the bullies are right, or accepting that you're going to feel like this forever. What this means is accepting that you're different and *using* it.

AND HOW IT STILL HAPPENS

For better or worse, as we navigate our way through the moral minefield of our childhood, we have certain ideals and stereotypes of bullying implanted from various mediums. This can be from our parents, from media influence, from teachers and sometimes from our peers. This kind of 'passive absorption' has both its good points and bad points. On the one hand, we are informed and we grow up with prior knowledge of bullying and its effects, a key and crucial point to stopping this kind of behaviour in its tracks.

As we mature, the more we learn how our actions affect others, however innocuous, the more we learn to desist from those that might harm or cause stress to others. On the other side of this coin though, negative behaviours are passed on by our forebears. The sins of our ancestors become the sins of our sons and daughters. From this, we as a society pick up all kinds of nasty habits. The 'it's all part of growing up' argument, when it comes to the subject of bullying, for example, is in itself a bad habit that people need to grow out of, like picking your nose on the bus. I cannot stress how damaging this can be, especially when this kind of attitude is promoted not just by parents, but by teachers and healthcare professionals, too.

'It's all part of growing up.' While I have done my best, thus far, to try to be at least partly impartial when it comes to the subjects covered throughout this book, I can do very little to hide my disdain at this contemptible turn of phrase. The easiest thing to liken bullying to, in defence against this kind of argument, is childhood conjunctivitis. (This legitimately, if not literally, came off the top of my head. The top of my head is a strange place.) A couple of my siblings and I contracted this during childhood. It's very common in children, and is usually quite mild and easily treatable. However, what it isn't, is pleasant. It's painful and uncomfortable, and if left untreated can cause blindness – in fact, it's the third most common cause of blindness worldwide.

No doctor in their right mind, on admission to a doctor's surgery or place of practice, would defer treatment with the statement, 'It's all part of growing up.' That would be barbaric, and would also be in breach of the Hippocratic Oath. While teachers don't make this kind of oath, it is part of human nature that humans want to help each other. The world is not a cold, dark place; it can be very easy to see the negative in the world, but that's just a product of our evolution. As we were evolving, if we remembered and dwelled on the negative, we were less likely to overlook something that could kill us. That was fine then, but in modern day life, we're not likely to bump into a natural predator on every corner, so this kind of behaviour simply doesn't serve us well anymore.

Bullying is not always as 'in your face' as modern media would have you believe. The 'being pushed in the locker room' scenario, the abject name-calling and this kind of situation does happen, but it's not as common as is often portrayed. There are many types of bullying, some of them physical and hurtful, some of them considered, sly and devious. Bullying in adulthood is generally slightly different to bullying in childhood – a bully who resorts to physical abuse in adulthood risks being reprimanded by the police, with a possible fine or jail term and a criminal record. Hence adult bullies, especially adult bullies in the workplace, will tend to use more subtle methods to 'get at' their victims, and will either stick to verbal abuse or make it look as if they were provoked when it comes to physical abuse. As the nuances of adult bullying are a little different from bullying in children, I'm going to list various types of bullies and their behaviours instead:

- **The Passive Aggressor:** This person is rarely negative to your face, but you can be sure they are always waiting for you to trip up. They don't talk about you in front of you, but you get the niggling feeling that you're the subject of talk behind your back. They always have a sneer ready for you when you stumble. They rarely, if ever, talk to you – more than this, their entire body language serves to alienate you. In a group conversation, they will always stand with their back to you in a way that serves to exclude you from the circle of conversation. When they do talk to you, their words are careful and considered and they will highlight at any opportunity that you 'don't belong'. They are the pinnacle of passive aggression. It can be difficult to ascertain whether the aggression is targeted at you; this is the essence of passive aggression. It can seem transient, like it's not aimed at one person in particular. To see whether it's targeted at you, watch how they behave around other people. This kind of person thrives on seeing that their actions are having an effect – if you take them as trivial, they tend to sulk and will ignore you completely, except for a few choice contemptuous looks. Ignoring is usually the way to deal with these bullies, as they thrive on reaction to their efforts – if there is no reaction, sometimes they can change track.

- **The Victim:** Playing the persecuted in this situation, this person is possibly one of the most dangerous types of bully and very definitely one of the most likely to lead to physical violence. If, or when, this happens (and if this kind of bullying isn't nipped in the bud, it will), the kicker is that there is a pretty good possibility that *they'll make it look like your fault*. When it's your word against theirs, and when someone is so proficient at playing the victim, it can be very difficult to redeem yourself. I've only been in this situation a couple times, and whenever anything happened or I retaliated, I always got the blame. Whatever you do, however much you are goaded, don't rise to the bait and never stoop to their level – you won't win; violence and anger only beget more of the same. Tell someone, make sure they keep it discreet, and try to make sure you're not alone together at any point.

- **The Egotist:** The Egotist is a conceited character, and you can take solace in the fact that if you are singled out by this type of bully, it's because you're better than them in some way. They will be merciless in terms of their assault on others who challenge their ego. This type of bully will likely be used to getting what they want, showered with praise growing up, so anyone who they feel is a danger to their lifestyle is an instant threat to be dealt with. The egotistical bullies I have met (there have been a few, but there's one that sticks out like a sore thumb as being an archetypal egotistical bully) were base and animalistic. They were defending their territory. Steer clear of these types, and keep conversation light and away from them as a subject whenever you must converse. If you're in a work environment, be pleasant and involve them in group conversation where possible. Sometimes this type of bullying may be rooted in a simple inability to relate to others without centralising subjects on their own person first, like a kind of buffer. Let it be known that you're a separate person, with your own qualities and idiosyncrasies, not a predator or a challenge.

- **Jekyll and Hyde:** This description actually encompasses two similar but also very different types of bully. The 'Jekyll and Hyde' persona will either be entirely pleasant when it's just you two, and then horrible when they're with their friends, or vice versa. The dynamic is the same, however. Welcome to the old cliché of Mr Hyde and Dr Jekyll (doctor's title optional). I once had a 'friend' who was nice as pie when it was just us chatting, but when his friends were about, he was all sneering and name-calling. Later on, he asked me not to talk to him when anybody else was around, so he wouldn't be 'seen with me'. It took a while for the penny to drop, but I eventually cut contact. I have seen him since and he's a different person now, so I'm not going to hold a grudge, but at the time I felt worthless, inadequate and defunct. The ironic thing about these feelings was that this type of person cares deeply about popular opinion of themselves. They will go out of their way to make sure they are viewed in a certain way. This type of bully is very common in later teenage years, and you may observe them making an appearance when you're the newcomer in a group of people. It's important that these people know how they can impact, as they often deem their actions harmless or inconsequential. As in every scenario, make sure you tell someone who can deal with this matter, and not just for the sake of retribution but because the chances are if the person acts pleasantly in one scenario and not in another, they know their actions are inherently wrong.

- **The Mercenary**: Always a follower, never a leader – this is the pathos of The Mercenary. They are in it for the protection and often simply to save the skin on their own backs by drawing attention away from themselves. Never alone, this type of bully will always be a sidekick, or one of a number thereof, to another bully. The one good point about this kind of bully is that when the alpha-bully – their foundation – falls, they will always crumble. When you tell someone about the main bully in a group, it's important to include their 'henchpersons' in the equation, lest they slither off and join another, equally damaging, group. Often in this situation, bringing the matter to someone's attention can help the person or people in question focus their actions towards 'fitting in' in a more positive sense and start to even lead in certain situations rather than simply living a life of perpetual following.

- **The Open Assailant:** The most dangerous type of bully, this person thinks they will never face retribution or rebuttal for their actions. Without any care for the feelings or emotions, or indeed well-being of others, they act recklessly and without regard. If left unchecked, they can ruin lives without even bothering or sometimes even realising. They lack any kind of empathy. When it comes to this type of person, you absolutely must tell someone, and tell them as soon as possible.

Very often people will say that they are 'just playing' or 'just messing about' when exhibiting bullying behaviour, and this is why it's very important to make sure you let it be known when someone's behaviour makes you uncomfortable *in the first instance*. There are ways to do this without being aggressive.

I've read some truly awful advice on dealing with bullies, from shouting 'No', or 'Help, I'm being bullied' to alert other people, to verbally beating down the bullies, thereby putting them in their place, to learning a martial art so you can go all *Karate Kid* next time the bullies strike. First off, shouting a bully down is always a terrible idea, for a number of reasons: one, you're actively establishing yourself as a threat, and two, shouting is a surefire way to kick somebody's fight-or-flight reflex into gear – whether they are the antagonist or not, this is a bad thing, as people don't think clearly under the influence of adrenaline, and the situation is much more likely to lead to physical violence. Three, you're ticking a box – congratulations, you just gave a bully verbal (and quite loud) confirmation that their behaviour is eliciting the desired reaction. Antagonising them or verbally beating them causes the same confrontational reflex and is also stooping down to their level. Besides that fact, it's also wrong. If you're reading this, the chances are you're not a kid anymore, and as you mature you realise that the world isn't neatly segregated into goodies and baddies. If a person is bullying because they're losing control in their own life and trying to claw it back through antagonistic behaviour, how much is hurting them really going to help? This type of behaviour should stay confined to Hollywood movies, where life is neatly sectioned into 20-minute or so scenes.

Throughout this chapter, I've spent most of the time talking about how to avoid aggressive behaviour when dealing with bullies. This may come across, at first, as being a little odd. I mean, if a bully is being aggressive first, why not fight fire with fire? If you want a four-word reason as to why this is a really, really bad idea, you just need to look at the wording of the expression I just used. *Fight fire with fire*. In what universe has this ever been a decent firefighting strategy? You don't see firefighters running into burning buildings equipped with flamethrowers. On a serious note though, if you decide to take this route, and 'fight fire with fire', return aggression with aggression, the result will play out exactly as the expression suggests. Everybody will end up getting hurt – you and the bully – and the only way it will stop is when there is nothing left. There is enough violence and aggression in the world; it doesn't need any more.

A lot of movies and TV programmes advocate martial arts or self-defence techniques in dealing with bullies, but these miss the point time and time again. Martial arts, in particular, teaches you how to defend yourself in such a way that you become confident enough that, usually, you won't have to use what you've learned. Would-be assailants often prey on those weaker than themselves, and seem to sense when you can handle yourself. Along with my family, I did Taekwondo for about six years, and I can't recommend this martial art enough, but not for the obvious reasons. It taught me discipline and self-control, it taught me how to stay calm in dangerous situations, and it taught me what self-defence really stands for – defending others or yourself in situations that can be diffused in no other way, and not for settling scores.

There are certain methods for dealing with bullies that are somewhat of a mixed bag, however, and everyone who has been bullied at any point in their life has probably heard, most likely from an outside party, the line 'just ignore them'. I have a special kind of hatred for this advice, not just because it has become such a cliché, but because *sometimes it works*. It's the sometimes that is the problem; it's become something of a blanket statement, and a large portion of the time it doesn't work. The problem is that it relies on the victim simply phasing back into the crowd and taking themselves off the bully's (or bullies') radar. When you're on the autism spectrum, 'blending into the crowd' is not the easiest thing. While standing out in a crowd in later life may be great, it renders this strategy almost completely useless when you're young. I'm in no way saying confrontation is the way forward, nor am I saying that this never works. It's just that people with an ASD tend to see the world a little differently, and bullies are pros at picking up the little nuances that make people unique and using them as targets. It works as an addition to other methods, the first and foremost being to tell someone, but waiting for that fire of terrorisation and intimidation to burn itself out usually isn't the best strategy, especially as some people are experts in finding the fuel wherever they can get it.

CONFIDENCE IS KEY: NIPPING BULLYING IN THE BUD

There came a point in my life where I simply stopped getting bullied. It was less of a paradigm shift and more of a change in attitude, but it wasn't in any simple way – I didn't just wake up one day and decide I wasn't going to take it anymore. Bullying relies on the ethos of 'the hunter and the hunted'. For a person to intimidate someone, they must pick someone who can be intimidated, or there is no pay-off, no effect to their cause, if you will.

Since I wrote the prequel to the book you're reading now, *Freaks, Geeks and Asperger Syndrome* (quick book plug there – I hear good things), a number of things happened, some good and some bad. One of the most notable things that happened was that unfortunately, throughout my teenage years and up until the age of about 18 I was attacked a fair few times. As a teenager, people seemed to get that I was different almost instinctively. Fair enough – by that point, I'd grown entirely comfortable with being a little different and wasn't scared to dress a little differently or act out of sorts, but I swear there were times when people could *smell* it. (So okay, showering never seemed like much of a priority when I was a teenager, but that's not what I mean.) The first time it happened, it knocked my confidence – I was scared to do much of anything. I was scared to go outside, so I stayed in a lot, and when I did go outside, everyone was a would-be aggressor. My anxiety knew no bounds; groups of kids, old ladies, anyone near me would be enough to make me panic. It was only after it happened a couple times that I started to realise that humans aren't made of glass. I ended up in a bit of a state, and still have a couple scars, but after that, the opposite happened. I didn't lose confidence, I *gained* it.

Now, I'm in no way suggesting that you'll be fine after a few fights. My reasoning lies in what happened afterwards, or rather what didn't, as it hasn't happened since. In gaining that confidence, learning how to approach people, I learned to avoid fights and prevent confrontations from leading to violence. Being targeted has a lot to do with confidence, or often the lack thereof. Humans are much more animalistic than we give ourselves credit for; we still pick up on lack of self-assurance, and there are certain types of body language that aggressors use to label someone as a would-be target. The kicker lies in the fact that the introverted behaviour caused by the bullies often leads to further bullying, because it confirms the victim's status as a target. Recovery takes time and often involves a lot of 'faking it'. The trick is assuming an air of confidence, even if it's a fake one at first. Over time, you start to learn positive behaviours that stick, and those habits that were at first contrived become real.

Both recovering from past events and removing yourself as a potential victim in the future aren't easy feats; and do take heed when I say that there is both no easy fix and no foolproof solution. The advice given here works for me, and it's been garnered from self-reflection, talking to a lot of people who've been in the same situation, both on and off the autism spectrum, and a little more life experience than I would've liked. There's no single solution to these kind of problems, and each situation should be handled sensitively. Many ways of deterring confrontation are rooted in body language: innocuous little changes to the way you hold yourself when you walk down the street, your tone and mannerisms when you meet someone, even down to that kryptonite of every autistic person, eye contact.

When a subject involves or causes fear or intimidation, a lot of people develop bad habits very quickly. One of the most prominent, unhealthy, and above all, very common ones is 'shrinking'. In the animal kingdom, some animals will puff their chest out, for example, to make themselves look bigger. Some people will do the opposite – they will attempt to 'shrink' themselves to appear less threatening or less prominent to would-be predators or bullies. People will withdraw into themselves, becoming more and more introverted so as to attract less attention. They diminish their persona so as to become as unobtrusive as possible, and in doing so, their quirks and qualities diminish too. I've been in this situation and it's barely an existence. It can only end badly, one way or another.

Often people on the autism spectrum bottle things up – hell, a lot of people do in general. When you feel you have to shrink who you are so drastically, that metaphorical bottle which stores all your stresses, your trials and tribulations shrinks with you, and it can only either shatter or blow its top. Either way is messy; this simply isn't the way to deal with things as you risk hurting yourself or others. If you're reading this and you feel this is you, talk to someone. If you feel you can't, take small steps first. Helplines help. While they can seem overly impartial, sometimes talking to someone who you don't know can help a little; just putting a situation into words can make it a bit more coherent, and often, from this, solvable. When you can, tell someone – when you're bullied as an adult, consequences can include more than just a slap on the wrist. If you're bullied near where you live, talk to the local council and the police, on a one-to-one basis or with someone else if you can't do it alone. If you're friendly and explain the situation, they will be willing to help. If it's happening in the workplace, bring it to your supervisor's attention, or if that doesn't work go higher up, and throw yourself into your work. Let the company you're working for know that if they leave the situation as it is, they risk losing a good employee.

Of course, there are positive ways to help with bullying, and to take yourself off the radar as a victim. We give away far, far more than we realise by virtue of body language, and vocal tone and volume. Once you realise this, you can start to be a little more self-reflective and begin to use these facets to your advantage.

We 'read' people's body language instinctively. Body language encompasses a myriad of different actions, largely confined to the unconscious side of the mind. It comprises our position in space and how close we are to someone or a group of people, our facial expressions and the way we hold ourselves (i.e. how we sit, stand and gesticulate). It even extends to how we interact with objects in our environment and less noticeable aspects of our personage, such as breathing and perspiration. A person sitting with their arms crossed portrays themselves as closed, and when someone is looking down or has their back turned to a crowd, they show themselves as unapproachable. This isn't, in itself, bad – it's also an incredibly useful thing to note if you're reading or doing something where you don't want to be approached, for example. However, a few subtleties in our body language betray a lack of confidence, very slight though they are. Downcast eyes belie a position of self-assurance; hunched shoulders are a sure sign of a lack of confidence. Bullies pick up on this – they see a lack of confidence as weakness. Often the aggression stems from a lack of self-esteem; aggressors pick up on their own shortcomings in other people and unconsciously attack them, thereby feeling as if they are making progress with their own problems. It's a self-perpetuating cycle, as when this doesn't work it just causes more anger.

When you turn these linguistic devices of the body on their head you can start to play about with how people perceive you. Good posture doesn't just mean you're less likely to have back problems in later life. When your shoulders are back, you're not hunched over and when you're sat with your feet apart from each other, you're seen as more open and confident. It's worth picturing how you look when you hold yourself in a certain way, or from an outside viewpoint. When you portray confidence, you remove yourself as an easy target in that you cease to exhibit what bullies view as weakness.

Unfortunately, eye contact is a key point when it comes to body language, too. I spent a lot of time when I was younger practising both in a mirror and on other people. It sounds odd, practising eye contact in a mirror, but I found it genuinely helped. Other people have found success in other ways, such as focusing on the bridge of people's noses. There are a lot of resources for parents and carers for helping children on the spectrum improve eye contact, but not a lot on helping adults with autism improve their eye contact themselves. Improving eye contact comes through practice, but there are ways to do this without causing undue stress and anxiety. Remember when you start out to take breaks – my eye contact is good, but I make sure I am always doing something where I can pause quickly when I'm talking to someone. A quick look out of the window, a look at your phone (but do be careful when you do this – looking at your phone mid-conversation can make you seem both closed and disinterested) can be enough to 'reset' the feelings of anxiety that are inherently associated with eye contact in ASD. In particular, remember to choose your battles wisely! Eye contact in a work interview is far more important than a meal with friends. Learn to prioritise – you'll find it helps.

Being assertive or showing assertiveness involves exhibiting confidence without being aggressive. It involves a myriad of different tricks, such as keeping a calm and even tone when speaking while maintaining just the right amount of eye contact, and utilising the body-linguistic devices I've described previously. The point is, it's not easy, at least at first. When we talk about assertiveness in general, we tend to talk about it as a side-effect of other characteristics. It usually comes packaged in the same sentence as 'successful', and people often talk about it in relation to heads of business, key musicians or people in leadership roles. We don't generally talk about it in and of itself, mainly because it's such a conglomerate of different attributes that it's very difficult to 'manufacture'. It can be done, however; it simply takes practice to do. Ironically, assertiveness begets assertiveness – the more life experience you gain, in particular positive experience, from asserting yourself in real-life situations, the more you will feel comfortable acting in a way that begets that kind of experience.

The *Oxford Dictionary* definition of 'assertive' is written as 'having a confident and forceful personality'. 'Forceful' is a big word in this case; to force something is to push or coerce someone or something into acting in a certain way. Being assertive is far from pushing someone into doing something, but is acting in such a way that people want to work with you, not against you. It isn't based exclusively around being friendly, but as the expression goes, 'You catch more flies with honey than vinegar.' Manners cost nothing, being friendly is free, and that brings us to another important point when it comes to assertiveness and bullying. There are a lot of articles written based around 'killing bullies with kindness'. This doesn't work in and of itself, otherwise I'm pretty sure we'd have a national hug-a-bully day by now, but it does work well when it comes to being assertive, especially in the case of bullying.

I have to stress – and I do hope, dear reader, that you take heed when I say this – that while being friendly isn't intrinsically linked with being assertive, not everything we do as humans has to be to gain something. On the most down of days, all it has taken is a passer-by to smile at me to brighten my mood and stop the day from becoming a write-off.

There have been a number of times when taking a different tack and being friendly has helped when I've been close to conflict situations in the past. One was when a few people in a group walking the same way as me were shouting things at me on the way home. I slowed down, then turned around and walked towards them, stopping to ask one of them for the time. Walking through the middle of them, I carried on and then turned down a side street to get back on my original route home. The key point is, you change the script. You can picture the usual situation. A person is followed home by a group of antagonists who are shouting abuse. They keep their head down and maybe walk a little faster. They may take a side street, where they may or may not be followed. If they break into a run, the chances are a chase ensues. Often, all it takes is change in a few key parameters to alter the outcome.

Assertiveness is a great thing and is a key factor when it comes to success in a number of situations, but there is something to bear in mind – if you're being assertive, you had better damn well make sure you're right. Being assertive is pushing forward a key point or points to sway a person to your way of thinking, so if the point you're making is wrong, you risk making other people wrong too, and assertive wrong people can be very dangerous people. Whether wrong or right, make sure you choose your battles wisely, too. If you're constantly consciously assertive (try saying that ten times fast) then you risk becoming insufferable. Identify people you are comfortable around, and take a break now and again.

Being confident and being assertive are different things in the sense that you can be passively confident, but being assertive involves asserting the points you want to get across, or even just asserting your very presence. Don't be that person who always has to be heard above everyone else – nobody wants to be that person. The beauty of being able to be assertive is that your confidence grows simply by proxy; once you learn that your opinion is as important as everyone else's, you start to be comfortable simply just *being*. It sounds an odd turn of phrase, but think how difficult it is just to exist. How many places are there where you can just exist, and how many people are completely comfortable doing so? Look around now, and see how many people you can see consciously doing nothing other than just *existing*. That is a skill.

Aggression and assertiveness, while not being the most obvious of bedfellows, are not too far away from one another, and it is very important not to cross that line into aggression when being assertive. When you assert your views, there will always be people to whom they aren't agreeable. In this case, friction can occur, and how you deal with these differing views is important. It is often from these differing opinions, and poor reactions to them, that bullying can occur, in an almost banal manner. If these disagreements occur often, then they can spill over into a dislike of the person themselves. This can then manifest in an unsubstantiated disdain for someone, which plants the seed for bullying. Avoiding this kind of situation, and stopping assertiveness from switching up into aggression, involves accepting that everybody has their own opinion and that a lot of the time you are not going to agree with them. If you ever find yourself in the situation, especially in a position of leadership, where you disagree with someone's input, don't simply disregard them. Think back to how you felt when your opinion was just set aside, brushed away as if it meant nothing. Then, instead of doing the same, look at why you disagree. Break it down; is there anything constructive you can take from it? If you can take constructive input from both opinions you agree with and disagree with, you'll become a better person for it.

Boundaries are important when it comes to confidence and it's essential to know the difference between being confident and assertive and, well, simply being an asshole. There are a few important things to reflect on, ranging from passive body language to nuances of vocal tone and volume. Some of these are passive, others not so much, but all can be done subconsciously, and this is why it's important to make sure you're self-reflective when it comes to confidence.

Passive aggression is the expression of resistance to opinions, requests or the very presence of others while avoiding direct confrontation, and the chances are that this definition brought someone to mind while you were reading it. If it did, congratulations, welcome to the world of adulthood, pull up a chair and get comfortable. The thing is, when confrontation is handled improperly in the adult world, it can be disastrous, so a lot of people will choose character assassination or sabotage in the way of aggression instead. People will still often make the switch into aggression without realising, through shouting and aggressive body language. Passive aggression often leads to confrontation before either party has realised what happened. Often, passive-aggressive and aggressive behaviour is subconscious, so here are some things to look out for, beginning with the least obvious:

- **Getting territorial:** Sometimes, people can use invasion of personal space to assert their territory, or ironically, their own personal space. This is where passive-aggressive behaviour becomes interesting, in that this is a very animalistic reflex, and it is very often not directed towards anyone in particular. A great example of this type of territorial behaviour is on the subway, when people sit with their legs spread apart far wider than necessary, often at the expense of other people's space. Other times, especially in the workplace, people will 'loom' over someone to assert their dominance, making themselves look bigger while the other party feels smaller.

- **Shutting out:** This is quite a common technique and can often be done subconsciously. When a group of people are having a conversation, they tend to form a circle, as the most convenient way to converse with each other without someone being in the way. When someone isn't welcome within the conversation, they will form a barrier to shut out that person, effectively preventing their input to the conversation. It can also happen in a line of people, and often happens to newcomers within a group. If you keep an eye on a group dynamic, doing the opposite of this and making extra space for a new person to join in the conversation is a good way to make someone new feel welcome.

- **Interrupting:** A surefire way to completely belittle someone, this is often a tell-tale sign of passive-aggressive bullying, as there is a very poignant and loaded subtext here. When a person is interrupted often by the same person or group of people, it is a very pointed way of saying that their opinion isn't worth listening to and, by extension, that it didn't matter in the first place. It isn't worth confrontation in the first instance, but if this happens often, cut the conversation. If it's a work scenario, tell a supervisor or someone higher; otherwise, look at whether the person or people doing the interrupting are really your friends, and whether they're worth it. Whenever it happens, direct your attention to someone else and continue the thread of conversation or, if possible, leave and do your own thing. Make it known that you won't stand for it, but whatever you do, don't be belittled by it.

- **Squaring up for a fight:** This is getting past passive aggression to the point of open hostility, but often if the person is doing their level best to avoid confrontation, it can be done passively. This is a very definite territorial challenge, and generally can't be mistaken for anything but. How this is dealt with depends on the situation. If you're in a work environment, or a crowded public place, the best option is to either very consciously turn around and walk away, or fold your arms in front of you, keep your voice calm and level and talk it out.

- **Raising the voice:** Here we hit on flat-out antagonism, and it isn't pretty. When someone raises their voice towards you, they're usually squared up to you, or they will be. Keep your voice level and calm, turn slightly away from them and keep your hands clasped in front of you. This way, you're in a position of non-violence, but your hands are ready to come up if anything physical happens. If you can get away from the situation, do – at least at present, this situation is unlikely to end well and should be resolved another time when tempers aren't flared.

Often the best reaction to confrontation in this manner is to make sure that the temper tantrum doesn't elicit a reaction. Make light of the situation and walk away. You will always come across as the bigger person.

Be aware that this entire sub-chapter is just theory garnered over a number of years. It's anecdotal, circumstantial evidence, and what works for me might not work for you. Take who you are and how you react in situations into account, and keep in mind that building confidence doesn't just happen overnight. In years gone by, I was plagued by anxiety, and this was an almost omniscient barrier towards improving self-confidence. It took a great deal of time, a lot of self-reflection and a lot of studying of the way people look and move and talk, and even just hold themselves, before I developed habits that have now become pretty much second nature. I still get anxious; it's just that now it doesn't show in the same way as it did before and the less it shows, the more people treat you as a confident person, and the more people treat you as a person with confidence, the more you become that person.

5

GOING OUT AND STAYING IN

NEW PLACES AND NEW FACES

Going out into town for the first time was probably one of the headiest experiences of my teenage life. I was going out to socialise and to drink and dance. I felt like a night of respite from the autism spectrum. One of my teachers once told me in school that when it came to his classes, I should 'leave my autism at the door'. I felt as if this was the closest I was ever going to get. I was out with my older brother and it started well. We went to some awful place, with whatever chart music was sullying the speakers at the time blasting out at plane-engine volume, and semi-sozzled men and women littering the place like human confetti.

I stuck out like the sorest of sore thumbs. One thing I've gathered (and become more comfortable with in later life) is that whenever I try to dress normally, I still look somehow obtrusive. I went out in a shirt, tie, trousers and shoes. Looking back, the shirt was purple with velvet lining down the sides. The tie was white, with spider webs drawn on it, because, well, spider webs are cool. My trousers were held up with an ace of spades belt buckle, and the shoes, I can't even remember but I'm pretty sure they were drawn on too. One of the most beautiful aspects of autism, however, is that often people on the spectrum hyper-focus on whatever it is they are doing. If I am talking to someone or dancing, I have zero attention left to focus on people staring – I simply don't notice.

The night started, and ended, innocently enough. It was on the way home that things got 'interesting'. Both my brother and I ended up being attacked, and I spent the night in A&E having some particularly tricky stitches on both the inside and outside of my lip, after receiving a nasty cut on my head and a free lip piercing from some charmer with a sovereign ring on and a penchant for building materials (at least judging by the half-brick that was later introduced to the side of my head at painful velocity). I found out a lot of things that night, not least that lacerations on the lip bleed a lot more than you'd think, and hurt a lot less. (Although, since having my lips pierced professionally, I've found out that if the above situation happens when sober, the reverse is actually true.)

My first night out was pretty disastrous – there wasn't much that could go wrong that didn't. I didn't get my drink spiked, but I think that was mainly a side-effect of growing up in a big family – if you put something consumable down then you could bet if you took your eye off it for a second it would be good and consumed. In summary, I went out to an awful club, full of questionable people, and then got attacked on the way home...and I was hooked.

I learned that going out is like watching a film on double speed with the volume turned up. It's just flat out strange – things happen that generally wouldn't in real life, people shout a lot more, everything's louder and faster. You meet some people who become your best friends for just that night, and then you may never see them again. Sometimes you click with someone and you get to know them and become intimately involved with them in the space of hours. The good things seem like the best things that could ever happen, and the bad times the very worst. When you add autism into this heady mix, then each night becomes an adrenaline rush, with its own buzz and crippling lows.

Like any rush, going out, being sociable, 'taking a break from autism', with its alcohol and social hangovers, can be addictive. For a while it was. I became, in turn, an introvert who barely spoke and was always planning for the next night out, and a social butterfly – not quite the life of the party, but not quite the recluse either. I watched the way people worked. I watched these cogs in the form of people spin their way through the night as the hands of the clock marched forward in such beautiful faux harmony. The interplay between the partygoers was as much a dance as the actions of the people littering the dancefloor; the moves were just different and it was speckled with conversation. I used to sit and ponder on how things worked and try to reconstruct the different conversations I'd seen. It became a pastime, then it became a habit, then an obsession.

Now things are better, but for a while it became my only hobby, and that wasn't a good thing. I became socially addicted, which is a very odd thing for somebody with autism to become, but going out created a high. For people with autism or Asperger's Syndrome, the bar for activities that create an adrenaline rush is lowered. Some people need extreme sports to get a rush, but I just needed to go to a party. It was dangerous; I felt as if I could be 'found out' at any point – and sometimes I was. People would pull me up on certain habits, certain idiosyncrasies related to Asperger's Syndrome. Sometimes the crowd would get too much or I'd misread someone's body language or say something wrong. There would be these awful moments where I'd say something completely out of context, because I'd blurt out something and just assume everybody knew what was going on in my head. There followed these all-consuming black holes of conversation which became the perfect breeding ground for anxiety. The thing is, the fear and anxiety I felt at such moments were unfounded – everybody has these moments at some point. Fair enough, my 'awkward moments' were rooted in different circumstances, as not everybody has an ASD and the problems with theory of mind that accompany it. The trick, I found, is in the recovery; I spent hours thinking of conversational tangents to bridge off into should these moments occur, and they worked. If you can pick the conversation up quickly enough, you can stop these 'conversational wormhole' moments in their tracks.

For me, following a night out there were two separate types of hangover. First, there was the obvious hangover, from too much imbibing of that hopeful social lubricant, alcohol. I've never been a huge drinker; I've had nights where I've drunk far too much, but these were more the exception than the rule, and the hangovers that followed served as a painful reminder not to do it again, at least until I forgot the accompanying symptoms. Second, and compounded by the first type of hangover, there was a hangover that was a little more social in nature – and I don't mean it'd wander up, shake hands and introduce itself.

'Running an emulator' carries with it its own detrimental after-effects. It is sociality by memory; there involves a constant drudging up of social nuances and rubrics that takes its toll over time. A 'relaxing drink with friends' isn't relaxing at all, but involves a complicated recalling of faces, body language, different expressions and social aphorisms. It can be enjoyable, sure, in the same way that someone can enjoy work, as I do in writing this. But as is the case with too much work, if you run an emulator for too long you risk burning yourself out, and after I'd been out I'd spend whole days where I'd shy away from any human contact completely. I still get these 'social hangovers' to some degree, but I'm a lot more open about autism now, and I was slightly less so back then. Now, people give me the space I need and are pretty understanding. Back then, nobody understood how I could go from being this eccentric character in the thick of the party to maintaining complete radio silence.

There's a definitive, yet subtle knack to knowing when to bring up autism spectrum disorders when you're out. I've known a lot of people who bring it up far too much, and some who would have benefited from drawing attention to it. People I've met have been far more accepting than I ever would've thought, but this can often be both a curse and a blessing. Sometimes it can seem like acceptance at the cost of downplaying some very real issues. Friends will, and should, accept you for who you are, so announcing your ASD to the world is often moot and will likely be met with an air of flippancy. Humour works in a lot of situations, so if you can joke about it, especially with people who aren't too aware of autism and its repercussions, most of the time it will be well-received. Humour is the great rejoinder; it brings people together and sheds a little light on the unknown.

Part of the reason we are so scared of going out is that we over-analyse things. People on the autism spectrum may have more of a propensity to do so, in that we pick out the small details, but it is a problem far from confined to those with autism. It almost seems to be an old evolutionary throwback – we focus on a thousand things that could go wrong, and thus shy away from any kind of confrontation, even positive. What we overlook is that a lot of things can go right too. Simply put, if we stay away from potentially negative situations, we feel that we lock ourselves away from harm. In reality, we stymie our ability to live our lives to their fullest degree. This sounds like the kind of thing you see on social media, usually with an unrelated picture of a sunset in the background, but it's also very true.

The struggle is real. We all struggle to make that social leap, whether we have autism, Asperger's, ADHD or are without any diagnosis. If there's one gargantuan myth that needs dispelling with speed, it is that people on the spectrum can't or won't socialise, or that their doing so is somehow tantamount to a removal of their diagnosis. I've had both of these misconceptions thrust on me in the past. It is more apt to describe sociality in people with ASD as being reconfigured, as opposed to simply 'switched off'. When we are young, our brain is hardwired to absorb and pick up languages subconsciously. As we become older and our brain's plasticity is reduced, this ability wanes. We must make a conscious effort to commit words and sentences to memory. People who aren't on the autism spectrum pick up social caveats naturally, in the same way, but learning social ethos, like learning a second language as an adult, isn't impossible – it is simply learned and recalled in a different manner.

Socialising and going out can be good, but it can also be terrible. Things can and do go wrong, and it's important to prepare for these eventualities. I've had some days and nights go horribly wrong, and even start wrong, but they could have been avoided with a little contingency planning. The thing is, people's plans do change, and you'll find yours do too. At least in terms of big events, whether it's for networking, making friends or otherwise, it's prudent to invite more people than are likely to turn up. The number of people that actually come varies depending on who you know, but in general, a lot of people will say they're coming when they've filed it in their mental compartments as 'maybe'. It can also be useful to have a 'back-up plan', be it staying in with a takeaway, having a gaming night, catching up with family or a friend you haven't seen for a while, anything. This helps avoid that lost, irritable feeling that is so synonymous with plans that have just gone completely awry, and stops you taking it out on those around you. It sounds bad, but often when I've been planning to do something and it falls through, I've ended up in less-than-coherent arguments with those around me, in particular my family or partner. It's important to catch these and nip them in the bud before they turn into something ugly. When plans change or fall through, remember that how you're feeling isn't the fault of the people around you. Try to rationalise it and work on more constructive ways to vent.

In summary, going out and meeting people, is one of the best and worst things you can ever do. It's a bit of an emotional rollercoaster, and often you won't feel fully in control, but if you ride it out you'll often have fun. Spontaneity is great, and it can be the kindling to the fire of a great day or night out, but it's crucial to make sure you're ready for anything if things go awry. Even the best contingency plans can fail, so it's important to have a get-out clause too. Always make sure you have the means to get out of a sticky situation. Often people in crowds don't think clearly and the herd mentality takes hold – groups of people can do things that the individuals involved wouldn't even think of doing separately. Sometimes you find yourself in situations you would really rather not be a part of and it is at these times that you need to make sure you're not stuck. If you go on an outing with friends, ask yourself a few questions. Where is it that you're going, and if you need to get away, can you? How far away from home are you, and can you get back if needs be? Do you have an emergency contact to call? These aren't things that need to be broadcast, but they're important things to think about before heading out. Simply having the option of leaving if something goes wrong often means you enjoy an outing more than you would otherwise. It's not pessimistic, it's realistic.

6

DRUGS: THE GOOD, THE BAD AND THE UGLY

THE CHANCES ARE THAT at some point someone, probably some shady-looking guy in a nightclub on a night out, will offer you drugs. People tend to become involved with drugs, if at all, during their teens, but it's by no means confined to that time. During my teens, I experimented with drugs - this chapter is not intended to steer you either away from or towards recreational drug use. That isn't to say I don't have my own opinions on the subject. People with Asperger's have an environmental proclivity towards depression, born of a feeling of 'living on the outside'. As I've struggled with these issues myself, and being diagnosed with bipolar disorder, I make a marked point of avoiding anything that may inadvertently affect my already somewhat disordered neurochemistry. However, having looked around at some research on the subject, there isn't all that much from a personal point of view. Just because a drug is included in here, it doesn't mean that I've tried it. I'm very careful with what I put into my body – when I was younger, I had some strange reactions to various pharmaceutical drugs and so I felt that when taking drugs for recreational reasons I'd have similar unusual effects.

Personal opinions aside, one of the most glaring reasons to give all due care and attention when it comes to recreational drugs is the inherent lack of regulation. As recreational drugs such as MDMA are Class A illegal drugs, ones that are shipped into or made in the UK are made safe only at the makers' discretion. That means you're never completely sure (and contrary to popular belief, neither is the person you get it from) whether what you're getting is actually active and pure, or whether it's safe or not – and sometimes it isn't. I've known a couple of people who died from badly made or poorly manufactured MDMA and it was more than enough to dissuade me from becoming involved in that scene.

I have heard so many arguments for and against drugs, but the fact is that anything, even if it's not physiologically addictive, can be addictive on a personal, psychological level. Humans can grow to crave something that makes them feel a certain way and this can quickly turn into a habit, which can turn into a full-blown addiction, especially if somebody already has a predisposition towards escapism in the first place. It can become a crutch, something that takes away the edge at times of difficulty, and when this happens, you're in trouble. There are too many variables, and each time you take something it is different to the last time. It depends on whether and what you've eaten, if you've had a drink, how much you've drunk, whether you're happy, sad, angry, bewildered or stressed, and that's just personal variables. It also depends on who you're with, where you are and what the music's like. Add to this the body's natural ability, or tendency, to develop an immunity to certain drugs, and you have yourself a crutch made of sticks and straw.

Drugs are generally split into two categories: 'hard' drugs and 'soft' drugs. They're split in terms of harmfulness to the users, judged by both toxicity and addictiveness. Soft drugs include cannabis, LSD and ecstasy, while hard drugs are things like cocaine and heroin. One of the biggest things to remember is that just because something is legal, it doesn't mean that it's safe. Some drugs, such as tobacco and alcohol, come between hard and soft drugs. Both are highly addictive and highly dangerous. Caffeine is also highly addictive, but its stigma has been all but removed because of its legality.

The world of drugs is a strange one. In an effort to make sense of this weird drug-based landscape, we're going to call on an old friend, the bulleted list. The list that follows is a rundown of the more common street drugs that are around, their synonyms, effects and risks. Some of it is based on my own experience, in one way or another, some of it on other people's experience, and some of it on research. As there are a great many resources online about the good and bad points of recreational drug use, I'm going to try to describe the various street drugs, specifically the five main drugs you're most likely to be offered when you're out – ecstasy, ketamine, speed, cannabis and cocaine – with relation to their effects on an autistic individual. Anyway, down the rabbit hole we go.

- **Ecstasy** – *MDMA, Es, Mitsubishi, XTC, Mandy, Molly, Mum, Dad, pills*

Ecstasy is taken in pill form and is an 'upper'. The pills are often given their names by the image stamped into the front of the pill. It has strong links to dance music because it was used to help people survive the all-night party scene of the late 80s/early 90s. It makes people feel awake, invigorated and refreshed, as if they have the energy to do anything. Sounds, smells and everything else are much more finely tuned. Often it has the side-effect of causing feelings of love and adoration for other people. Generally, it takes about 20 minutes or so to 'come up' and tends to last about three to six hours.

If the positive effects were the only effects it had, I'm pretty sure everybody would be taking it all the time. Recently there have been trials of MDMA for use in people with post-traumatic stress disorder, with limited results. However, these aren't the only effects. While I must stress, for the purpose of impartiality, that these effects don't happen all the time, they sometimes do, which means every time you take a pill, you make a gamble.

One of the short-term effects and one of the most noticeable from an outsider's perspective is an onset of anxiety. As anxiety is 'a feeling of worry, nervousness or unease about something with an uncertain outcome', the chances are high that if you have an ASD, you've already had some form of acute anxiety before. Obviously, everyone is anxious at some point, but if you're more prone to anxiety, adding outside influences such as ecstasy to this can certainly compound the issue. This added anxiety also raises the chance of a panic attack or meltdown, and as the effects of ecstasy can also cause confusion, people often end up less than able to deal with these attacks.

From an outside perspective, to someone sober, the effects of ecstasy aren't pretty. The drug generally results in a rise or fall in body temperature, causing sweating or the chills, and shaking. This, coupled with occasional involuntary muscle tension, causes gurning – the rolling of the tongue, clenching of the jaw and licking of the lips – to create a not altogether pleasant look. On top of this, the tendency to become more conversational and lose any or all sense of personal space means that it's much, much easier to get into fights.

One of the most notable and most talked about side-effects of ecstasy, however, is the comedown. MDMA acts on serotonin, a neurotransmitter within the brain thought to play an important part in mood. It comes in leaps and bounds and the elevated serotonin levels go towards causing the pleasurable feeling and oneness that are so associated with the drug. Afterwards, people can experience two or three days of depression, often called a comedown. One possible explanation for this is that the brain takes a while to regulate after being bombarded with serotonin, which could be what causes what is often known as the 'midweek blues', due to people's tendency to take ecstasy at the weekends. Restoration of proper serotonin levels can take 48 hours or even a week, depending on the person. Ecstasy has been linked to long-term depression in past studies and it could be down to some people's inability to reach homeostasis, or proper balance. If there are already pre-existing depressive tendencies in users prior to taking it, then usage could compound these.

The most important thing to remember with ecstasy, as with anything, is not to take it lightly and to be aware of the risks involved when doing so. There are a notable number of deaths each year from ecstasy. This is partly because when you take a pill, you never really know what's in it. You'll hear people talking about a certain type, such as 'sharks' or 'love hearts', but at the end of the day, the only discernable difference between one pill and another is the colour and the stamp. If you do take it, make sure you have eaten and slept properly beforehand. Both of these affect serotonin production and will help speed up and improve recovery. On top of this, make sure you don't mix the drug with alcohol.

As ecstasy causes dehydration, it's important to make sure you drink enough water, but don't drink too much. An excess of water can cause death by dilutional hyponatremia, or low sodium concentration in the blood caused by water intoxication. In short, if you're not careful, you can end up drinking yourself to death. Obviously, the amount of water varies on the situation and ambient temperature, but a good ballpark figure is around a litre of water every couple hours. If you drink isotonic drinks, they will help replace some of the electrolytes lost when sweating. Make sure you sip drinks and don't just gulp them down.

● **Ketamine** – *special K, donkey dust, K, vit. K, super K, ket*

Ketamine was first developed as a veterinary anaesthetic in the 1960s, and moved into human use as it had fewer side-effects than its common predecessor, PCP. It anaesthetises the body without affecting the respiratory system, and is therefore used in a number of minor operations and was deployed as a field anaesthetic during the Vietnam War. Interest grew in its use as a recreational drug and there has been a resurgence of people taking it in recent years. It's sometimes added to MDMA to change its effects and can be taken in powder form, or more rarely pill or even liquid form, which is injected. It's very commonly snorted, in lines or off a key.

First of all, let's talk about the effects of ketamine. As a general anaesthetic, it has the effect of anaesthetising one to the outside world, creating a disconnection between body and mind, an effect that can last from around 20 minutes to an hour. It can leave you feeling completely relaxed and at peace. On top of this, ketamine can have hallucinogenic effects which can last from half an hour to several hours and can change the way you see and hear the world in the period the effects are active. People can often become completely immobile and enter a 'k-hole', frequently likened to a near-death experience.

There are a number of risks associated with taking ketamine. First and foremost, as ketamine was originally developed as an anaesthetic, the drug leaves the body vulnerable. A dulled pain response coupled with reduced motor coordination skills and disinhibition can leave you open to being hurt and not even realising it. As ketamine can leave a person completely incapacitated, it is also commonly used as a date-rape drug. You are leaving yourself completely open, and thus need to be immensely careful where and when you take it. As with many drugs, especially tranquilisers, it can also leave you confused and disoriented, and there is no 'off' switch you can use if you need to respond quickly, such as if you find yourself in danger.

At the time of writing, more and more research is coming to light about the effect of ketamine on the bladder and liver. In particular, when taking the drug, people feel the need to urinate frequently and urgently. If the urine contains blood or tissue, it can be an indication that the bladder wall is badly damaged and a bladder transplant may even be needed, or the urinary tract is affected and incontinence can occur. Before the research, however, there were long-term users hospitalised with abdominal pains referred to as 'k-pains' or 'k-cramps', and these people would often take ketamine to lessen the pain, compounding the problem.

Ketamine is a physiologically addictive substance and has the propensity to be psychologically addictive too. When someone is physiologically addicted to something like ketamine, however, they can often fool themselves into thinking that they just like it and the feeling it gives. The kicker is that, even though this may be true, there is no way to tell, and very often the body builds up a tolerance, so people need to take more and more to reach the same high. When people continue using something that is damaging their health and starting to encroach on the times when they aren't using it, this is when they need help the most.

- **Cannabis** – *weed, green, Mary Jane, marijuana, pot, grass, bud, draw, herb, skank, ganja*

Cannabis is a drug derived from the cannabis plant, with different types of cannabis often pertaining to different parts of the plant. The active ingredient is THC, or tetrahydrocannabinol. There has been massive debate in the UK in recent years as to the question of its legality and it's been recently legalised in many parts of America. Part of the argument for its legalisation stems from its effective use as pain and nausea relief in the treatment of advanced stages of some cancers, AIDS and multiple sclerosis, to name a few. It is taken in a number of ways and is often smoked with tobacco, a point which is frequently used in the arguments against its decriminalisation. It can be smoked in a joint with or without tobacco, filtered through water in a bong or cooked in or sprinkled onto food. When smoked, the effects are nigh on instant, whereas cannabis when ingested takes a little longer to kick in.

Cannabis has a number of effects, ranging from relaxation through to mild hallucinations (which are much less common). It can make you feel extremely relaxed and laid back. Stronger strains can have you laughing at nothing, confabulating about the most random of subjects and perceiving colours and music differently. The effects vary wildly from person to person and depend heavily on the type of cannabis and the way it is taken. After-effects of strong cannabis include a dry mouth, bloodshot eyes and a distorted perception of time, along with a huge reduction in reflexes. On top of this, cannabis tricks the brain into thinking you're hungry, which results in 'the munchies'. Be prepared to eat yourself out of house and home.

In recent years, cannabis has changed a little. When I was growing up, resin, also known as hash, was very common: a brown or black lump that is generally heated and crumbled into joints, bongs or brownies. Nowadays, green or skunk, dried buds and leaves of the cannabis plant, are much more commonplace and are stronger than they were in the past. It affects different people in different ways – for some people, having a smoke is an incredibly normal event, simply a way to chill out after a heavy day. The chances are these people have been smoking for a while and their bodies are more accustomed to the hit. Other people will become slow and lazy and the habit can consume them. Weed is less addictive than other drugs, but it can become psychologically addictive. I've seen it rule people's lives and become their only hobby, almost their entire *raison d'être*.

Weed carries its own set of negative effects. It can cause paranoia and exacerbate pre-existing anxiety. How the drug affects you depends on a whole plethora of variables, such as who you're with, how you're feeling at the time and what you've eaten. There are some studies that have linked cannabis to mental illness, and some that have undermined that link. If you're going to take it, then use your best judgement, educate yourself on the subject and keep in mind genetic predisposition when it comes to mental illness. If you have mental illness in your family, then it would be prudent at least to be wary when it comes to using the drug. In addition to these effects, cannabis does have a negative effect on memory retention and cognition. It doesn't help you when it comes to learning, so if you do smoke it, leave it until after work, college or university – you wouldn't come into work or college drunk, so for goodness sake, don't come in stoned either.

People have different tolerance levels when it comes to cannabis, and if you've been around anyone who smokes it at all, you'll hear the word 'whitey' thrown around a lot. To 'whitey' is basically to breach your tolerance for smoking weed. It can cause massive anxiety, paranoia, nausea and a feeling of being generally unwell – and feel unwell you will. Seriously, the colour will disappear from your face, hence the term, 'whitey' or 'white-out'. A very extreme 'white-out' culminates in vomiting, though often this is down to inhalation of too much tobacco very fast, for example when mixed in with weed in a bong. People will go 'past the point of no return' for a number of reasons. Sometimes it can be lack of knowledge of the various types and ways of taking it – some strains are much stronger than others and you'll get a much stronger hit from a bong than a joint, for example. Other times it's peer pressure – people will feel as if they have to 'catch up', in a similar manner to drinking alcohol with friends on a night out. Some people suggest sugary foods to remedy the onset of a whitey, but how effective this is isn't known, and there aren't likely to be any studies on this in the near future. Remember, less is more – if you feel as if you've had enough, don't let anyone push you past that. Once you're up, you can't just come down straight away, you have to ride out the effects.

A lot of the current literature on cannabis is somewhat one-sided. In recent years, it has seen publicity as both Disney villain and hero. Cannabis is not a wonder-drug that will enrich your life and cure cancer (though it has seen some recent success in certain trials). Neither is it an evil poison that will completely remove your will and status as a human being. If you smoke cannabis, it should be as a recreational habit, don't make it your life. If you start to feel as if you 'need' a joint and get cranky and irritable without it, the chances are you're developing an addiction. The same applies if you feel as if it isn't doing anything for you, but still take it, and then find you're having to take more and more – self-awareness is key. Exercise caution and educate yourself.

One last note – do remember that tobacco is an addictive substance. There have been no recorded deaths with cannabis as the sole cause, but there are around 100,000 smoking-related deaths in the UK each year. If you don't smoke cigarettes, but mix cannabis with tobacco, and you find yourself craving a joint throughout the day, there is a fairly substantial chance that it's the tobacco you're craving, but your brain hasn't made that link.

- **Cocaine** – *coke, Charlie, toot, blow, snout, sniff, rocks, C*

Cocaine, or coke, has long been glamourised and featured in Hollywood films as the drug of choice for the rich and famous. In recent years, prices have dropped and Joe Public, i.e. the general populace, has begun taking it, with increased imports coming in as demand increases. Coke creates a rush, a feeling of euphoria that is short-lived but highly potent. As the hit only lasts around 20–30 minutes, people need a lot to keep on top of their high. At around £30–60 for a gram, this can impact on your bank balance as much as anything else. The drug makes the dullest of events seem life changing, and your confidence soars. You'll become chatty and alert, the life and soul of the party. The thing is, everything is relative, and although you feel confident and alert, there's every chance you'll come across as loud, brash, arrogant and, well, a bit of an asshole.

Like a lot of stimulants, coke is an appetite suppressant and so regular users can become malnourished as the drug cuts out any sense of hunger. As a stimulant, it puts strain on the heart, so shouldn't be mixed with any other stimulants. Smoking cocaine's other form, crack cocaine – mixed from baking soda, coke and water – can cause damage to the lungs, bronchitis and chest pains. In addition to the bodily health concerns, long-term use can affect mental health, resulting in depression and, in extreme cases, drug-induced psychosis, a condition with symptoms similar to schizoid disorders.

- **Speed** – *whizz, phet, paste, base, sulph, billy, dexys*

Speed is a type of amphetamine, an addictive 'upper' that makes people awake and alert, at a cost. It turns the most introverted introvert into a chatty, extroverted partygoer. Often, people will take speed to stay awake when partying for days on end; after taking it, you'll feel as if you can dance forever and you'll be confident and bursting with energy.

Speed makes you do things with a quickness and can evade fatigue in a way that nothing else seems to. Speed tends to come in wraps, little balls of powder for around £10, and is taken in a number of different ways. It can either be rubbed onto the gums, snorted or even heated up and injected. Sometimes people 'bomb' it – roll it into a paper and swallow it. The effects last up to around six hours, but different ways of taking it often provide a different kind of high; if you bomb it, the effect will be pronounced but won't last as long. Snorting it will mean the body absorbs it much faster and the effects kick in much quicker.

There are a couple of side-effects to this sudden energy boost. You won't exactly find yourself wanting food, for example; speed kills the appetite, so much so that it was a chief ingredient in early diet pills, and some diet pills still contain legal variants of speed. You can become disinhibited, and if you mix speed and alcohol, anything can happen – rather than passing out, you may find yourself carrying on indefinitely and wake up the next day (or more likely, the night after, having stayed awake all night and slept the day through) in all manner of states. This disinhibition, alongside the new-found confidence, can turn you into everyone's best friend. The problem is, this isn't always reciprocated. People on speed can wax lyrical about anything that comes to mind, however horrendously dull. After about half an hour, they've recounted a good portion of their childhood in the most tedious of manners, all the while telling the nearest person they are just 'the best guy ever', even if they've only met them that night.

A couple of other side-effects have a little more of a physical manifestation. Shortly after taking it, people's mouths become incredibly dry, and no amount of liquid will moisten the Sahara Desert that has become their tongue. In addition, they may grind their teeth, causing long-term users to develop dental problems. As with MDMA, this can cause users to pull faces like contestants in a gurning competition. If you do decide to take this, be aware of this fact; speed is pretty far from a discreet drug and if you're in a place that's subject to random police searches, you're pretty much a grimacing neon 'search me' sign. Alongside this, people build up tolerance to speed pretty fast, so if you're not careful, you could end up with enough on you to be slapped with a 'possession with intent to supply' charge. The more you take, the more you need to take to get the same hit. On top of this, street speed is incredibly impure, with an average purity of just 5-10 per cent. You have no idea when you're taking it what the other 90-odd per cent is and, more importantly, how harmful or addictive it is. Some of the 'fillers' may be completely inactive, some may be addictive and some may be harmful.

While I said I'd try my best to stay impartial for the duration of this chapter, what I will say is that if you have heart problems, then avoiding speed may be for the better. Speed puts quite a strain on your heart and raises your blood pressure, so long-term use, especially with pre-existing heart complaints, can and likely will be dangerous. Some types of speed are stronger than others; in particular 'base', which produces a stronger hit and more intense symptoms, can place a great amount of strain on the heart. If you mix it with other stimulants, it can put extra stress on the body. Avoid other uppers like coke, MDMA or poppers, as these could bring on Serotonin Syndrome, a potentially fatal overload of serotonin within the brain.

The comedown from speed is not an enviable experience. Take a little lethargy, add some general feelings of being unwell and a dash of depression and possible paranoia and you've got a recipe for a pretty bad speed hangover. The symptoms that show depend on how much you've taken and for how long. As with alcohol, prevention is better than cure; make sure you stock up on vitamins and that you eat well both before taking it and afterwards. Like alcohol, however, there is no way to completely negate its effects – be very careful and do your research if you must take it.

7
SEX AND RELATIONSHIPS

THE WORLD OF DATING and relationships is a strange one, and each person's experience is different. I think it was when I started meeting people on dates that I first obtained a real love for people. One of my favourite words is 'philanthrope', sometimes still used as a term for someone with a genuine love for people. It's only when I started dating that I realised how different everyone is; everyone has their own story, shaped by both genetics and personal experience. In Asperger's there is a 'them and us' culture that has been propagated in recent years, and it is only when you start to question this by listening to what others have to say that this cultural non-sequitur is broken down.

Ever since I was young, I have always had problems with dating. This remains the case today; it's just that at some point the nature of those problems changed. When I was younger, people were a maze of different habits and idiosyncrasies and social ethos that I had absolutely no understanding of. I felt like a complete outsider; the world passed me by as if being viewed through a keyhole. Bits and pieces flashed by, but there was never enough to piece together a coherent social picture. Then, that fickle and beautiful thing, love, happened. I was spellbound by the dichotomy of it all – it was both the easiest and most comfortable and yet the most difficult thing I have ever come across. She was a girl a lot like me – an outsider, a wayward one, lost in a world that passed her by – and we both found solace in that. I have always written, and when I met her the words flowed easily. She was my muse. A little of that may still be present, or maybe today is simply a good day for writing, as the words are falling from my fingertips and adorn the page in their own neat order, as if sentient.

My first relationship was also my first 'heartbreak'. It ended fairly abruptly; we were too far apart. I would walk miles and miles in the dead of night to see her, but there was simply too much against us both. It felt almost tangible, a burning pain low in my chest, and my thoughts were consumed by her. Everybody struggles when it comes to love – it is the most natural and talked about of human conditions – but none, I think, more so than those on the autism spectrum. We are fixers; if something is broken, we fix it, but this device we use to explain the process of grieving when it comes to love, a broken heart, cannot be fixed. They say time heals all wounds, but wounds leave scar tissue too, and I hold the suspicion that we all carry the scars from lost loves. Sometimes people champion them, as war wounds from battles won, as in those brave ones who have escaped abusive relationships, and sometimes they are hidden away, too painful to talk about lest they remind us of a better time.

It is in loss that we fall on one of the biggest 'unwritten rules' of dating. We are not taught how to deal with loss when we are young. People may touch upon grieving and bereavement, but when it comes to losing someone we love, not through that most final of circumstances but through simply coming to the end of a relationship, people with an ASD are often the least well-equipped. It is the biggest of changes; often that person becomes a huge part of our waking life. We shape our life events around them, share our highest and lowest moments with them, and then they are gone, often very suddenly. It is well-known, and a crucial part of the diagnostic criteria for autism spectrum disorders, that people on the spectrum do not deal well with change, and a break-up can turn someone's whole life around.

Maybe it is the struggles that surround dating and relationships when it comes to people with autism spectrum disorders that propagate the myth that people on the spectrum are somehow loveless. Often it is believed that they lack the ability to be romantically involved with another person. To arrive at this, one strips away the entire ability to relate to another person on a romantic level, and this can almost be construed as offensive. A person on the autism spectrum is just as capable of love, trust, affection, or even simply lust or infatuation, as someone who has no diagnosis, or even no traits, of autism. Indeed, often the feeling is entirely magnified, as finding someone you can entirely relate to, especially on a romantic level, can be rare for those on the autism spectrum.

For me, being different, at first such a curse and a burden, became a great thing. When I found out I had Asperger's Syndrome I challenged the diagnostic criteria laid out before me. In doing so, I became a little better at alleviating some of the more debilitating parts of Asperger's in social situations. Still, I always stuck out as different. Initially, I used to hate this – whatever I did, I stood out like a sore thumb. In growing up, however, I grew more comfortable with this and over time even began to use it to my advantage. From then on, things began to snowball; I was meeting people and networking as part of my work in photography, and the dating side of things just seemed to come naturally. It seemed that the more I focused on my work, and everything but, the more the dating side of things just sort of happened. I'm no Casanova, but I do believe that sometimes things do just come naturally.

UPPING YOUR DATING GAME

A lot of people on the autism spectrum struggle with dating, and while there is a lot of information on the subject online, it's incredibly convoluted and opinions differ widely on the subject. There is still a stereotype of people on the spectrum as being rigid, awkward, somewhat boring individuals, and obviously in some cases this can be true, but not in all cases. Some people can be awkward, and some people can be rigid, but this is because these are ultimately human traits. Everyone is different, and even the folk who seem most uninteresting have their own stories – this is why the process of getting to know someone is so fascinating, and why you should never make assumptions about someone before getting to know them. There is a possibility that people with autism spectrum disorders have more trouble dating because there are so many subtleties involved – knowing when someone likes you, when it's the right time to make a move, what to say, knowing when someone is hinting at something. Understanding these subtleties is like learning a second language, and to be fair, it should be treated as such.

Subtlety is tough, but a big part of understanding subtlety is first being able to take constructive criticism and understand that it's not a reflection on your character, and second, being able to shrug it off. The world of dating and relationships is a scary place, especially when you first get feelings for someone, and even more so when you've known them as a friend previously. It can turn the most confident of people into rambling, incoherent, nervous wrecks. The problem is that for a lot of people with an ASD, it can become all-encompassing. With the ability of a person with Asperger's to hyper-focus on something, it can end up overshadowing much of their life. What seems to happen is that the more you focus on searching for a significant other, the more elusive they become. Therefore, a lot of people on the autism spectrum end up obsessing over finding someone to share their interests with. This can be unhealthy and just isn't conducive to getting a date. If finding a partner becomes someone's be all and end all, or the thing they strive for most, it puts a lot of pressure on potential partners to match up to expectations, and can be off-putting.

In the interest of honesty, I'm going to come out and say this straight – humans are superficial creatures. We make split-second decisions on people based on very little information, such as their facial contours or expression, and this is pretty shallow. However, when it comes to snap judgements on things like clothing, the conclusions are less shallow. How a person dresses, their posture and frame, together with their facial expression can give big clues as to how a person lives their life, and thus clues as to how they'd be in a relationship. This picture starts to break down under conscious scrutiny, because each person is different, but people subconsciously assess a person's appearance. A person's appearance accounts for a great deal, and people's reaction to it often change, depending on the situation. A person in jeans, trainers and a band t-shirt may be seen as easygoing and carefree, but wear this for a job interview and you're unlikely to get the job. At other times this works the other way around – wear a tux to go on a daytime shopping trip and you're likely to get a few funny looks.

Appearances aside, there are a few things that can be done to improve your chances. Make sure you shower regularly for starters – smell matters more in first impressions than we realise. It helps to be self-reflective in this case; notice how differently people can smell and gauge which scents are pleasant and which aren't. I can still identify different people by their various smells, which are sometimes as intrinsic to them as a photograph. Personal hygiene is important and adhering to this is something people often overlook when it comes to dating. When it comes to clothes, dressing smartly or casually is open to interpretation. There are clothes that feel nice and still look smart, and finding a balance between the two is very important. It is one thing looking presentable, but if you don't feel comfortable, it'll show.

Approaching people is something that everyone, with or without an ASD, has trouble with. There is a misconception from a lot of people within the world of Asperger's and autism that so-called 'neurotypical' people are social machines that simply know the right words to say to someone they've just met, or can walk up to a stranger and engage in the smallest of small talk until they get a date with someone. In general, everybody struggles with this – while I'm fairly sure there are those mavericks who can simply saunter up to someone and start a conversation without a second thought (if you'll excuse the alliteration), usually this isn't how it works. When you approach someone new for the first time, you have no idea what they're like, you have no idea what their views are, you have no way of even telling whether or not you will get on. Obviously, if you have a tendency to overthink things in general, then these kinds of issues are a breeding ground for anxiety. Anxiety, at its roots, takes the worst-case scenario as the most probable one. But generally the worst-case scenario is an unrealistic one, and even if it happens, things move on. You should never be afraid of looking like a bit of an idiot – it happens to everyone, and those who are able to laugh it off and move past it are the ones who fare best in the dating world.

The anxiety that appears to go hand-in-hand with the process of meeting someone for the first time, and in particular when the interest is romantic, is not something that goes away easily, but there are ways of dealing with it. First off, disclosure is a big subject people miss when it comes to anxiety and dating. You are in no way weak by feeling anxious when you meet someone new or go on a date. It's completely normal, but the way you bring up the subject is key; remember, the anxiety is not an excuse but a reason for certain behaviours, and once you've broached the subject, don't keep coming back to it. The same goes with an autism spectrum disorder – once you've disclosed it, the other person isn't going to forget, so the subject doesn't need to be brought up again.

There is no substitute for practice when approaching new people for the first time, and it takes a big push to make yourself do it. You keep replaying the worst-case scenario in your head, and then when you actually go over and say something, it isn't so bad. I was helped by the fact that I travelled around the country a lot, so I had a few 'neutral zones'. I'd take these as places where if something went wrong, it didn't really matter because nobody knew me. There was a very high chance I'd never meet those people again. If you do suffer from anxiety, you're probably familiar with what happens when meeting someone for the first time, even if it isn't in a romantic capacity. The symptoms are the same, it's just that often we are more aware of their propensity to embarrass us. Your heart starts pounding, as if trying to beat its way out of your chest. Your mouth goes so dry that even talking out loud is a problem, and you're sure that if you did, it would just come out as a wheeze – which is just as well, because your brain is so foggy that you can't formulate any proper words anyhow. Your palms are sweating, you're sweating. You start to reflect on everything you're doing. Do I look okay, is my posture right? Then just: 'Hi, how are you?' That's it. It doesn't make the conversation any easier, but at least you got there. It's something, and often a conversation will follow on from that.

Jumping into a conversation with the intent to ask someone out on a date can be a surefire way to get shot down. Try not to approach someone with just that intention; the conversation tends to seem empty and vacuous, because if you do this, you are basically making inane conversation until a time comes to ask about a date. Simply put, this is pretty shallow. People each have their own little habits and idiosyncrasies, and if you just dive straight in for a date, then you're either going to end up out with someone that you don't like very much, or you may come across as vapid or not invested in the conversation. Even if I fancy someone (though I can't say the word 'fancy' without feeling 16 years old again) or, rather, am attracted to someone, I try not to jump into a conversation with the idea of setting up a date, or at least not in such an obvious sense. If you just arrange a coffee or a drink without attaching the stigma of a 'date' situation to it, it takes away a lot of the expectation and pressure that come attached to the world of dating.

The question of what to talk about when spending time with someone you like is a difficult one. First off, greetings are a good start. Asking 'Hi, how are you?' is a pretty standard conversational opener, and it's a pretty decent one if you're leading the conversation. When you're out with someone for the first time in a date capacity, i.e. it's just you two and there are romantic intentions involved, it's important to remember that not every silence is an awkward silence. It's worth saying when you broach the subject of the autism spectrum that you might take a little longer to process things, as this can take a lot of the gravity out of so-called 'awkward' silence. People pause to think in general, it's nothing to worry about – don't be sorry about it if you take a little longer to process things. It is part of your personality and you shouldn't be ashamed about that.

A good thing to do is to find out what the other person likes and to play on that. Ask what kind of music they're into, what work they do, what kind of things they like to do in their spare time. If the conversation is going well, don't be afraid to move past small talk though – ask where they've travelled, if they'd like to, if they have any big dreams. Good conversation is a great skill and one that traverses many different aspects of life. Try to find common ground, subjects and activities that you both like. If asked, don't be afraid to talk about the subjects that are important to you, but don't go too far and hijack the conversation with talk on your specialist subject (if you have one). That said, don't be afraid to emote about activities and subjects you feel strongly about. Passion is a great thing, and it's sexy in any gender. Just make sure that what you're passionate about isn't something likely to be too contentious or cause friction. If your argument is on the merits of Neo-Nazism as a system of ethics, your date is going to turn into an argument pretty fast.

Body language is a whole other language, with its own regional quirks and dialects. It's an incredibly important aspect of human existence, and if you're on the autism spectrum, it's worth doing some research. The best way to describe it is through analogy – body language works in this way: if an area is cordoned off it repels curiosity, it beseeches people to stay away, but a simple arrow in its place invites exploration. Neither of these are physical objects yet they still have power, and they are still great devices in terms of influencing people. Very often, it's not what you say, but what you don't say, and there are a few non-verbal devices that work in dating situations to help you come across in a certain way:

- If you have your arms crossed, knees together and hands clasped, you risk showing yourself as closed off and lacking in confidence. Keep your feet and knees slightly apart when sitting, and avoid crossing your arms. Lean back at your leisure, but try not to slouch, and don't worry about leaning forward when gesticulating about something you're passionate about.

- If you keep your eyes up (without staring) you come across as more forthcoming, and if you look up and away when gesticulating during conversation it gives you time to think without coming across as overly shy or breaking the flow of conversation. Eye contact is an important factor in body language, but there are ways around difficulties with it. Try looking between the eyes or at people's mouths when they are talking. If you decide to go for full eye contact during conversation, then take breaks – look away, whether it be out of the window or into the background; this prevents staring and helps to avoid anxiety.

- If you lean in towards the other person very slightly when they are explaining something at length, it shows that you're interested in what they have to say. The same applies if the person is sitting across the table from you. This is where clasping your hands can be a good thing; if you're in a coffee shop or a restaurant, putting your elbows on the table and clasping your hands under your chin can be a good way of showing interest. A warning, though: this is where eye contact comes into play, as the same action while looking away tends to come across as bored or disaffected.

- Gesticulating in conversation is something that I personally do a lot; it emphasises points, can be a visual reminder of the conversation and shows passion. It can be a useful conversational device, but keep your movements tight and close to you in normal conversation, then be more fluid when talking about something important to you. Make sure your movements don't encroach on your date's personal space.

- When standing, while posture is important, you don't need to stand board-straight all the time. Stand however you feel most comfortable; I tend to shift my weight from one leg to the other. Try not to hunch your shoulders up – it can make you come across as uptight and uncomfortable. If you find it more comfortable putting your hands in your pockets than letting them hang, try just resting your thumbs on your pocket and keeping your fingers out. This makes you appear more approachable and friendly – people often 'talk' with their hands, so by hiding them you're cutting off a potential thread of conversation.

It's important to note that while you may feel unconfident at first, when you project yourself in a certain way, it has the effect of letting your particular attributes and positive points come through more. Behaviour that starts off as contrived in the first place becomes real; this is a process known in psychology as behavioural activation (though I am over-simplifying the term). Earlier, I likened body language to a verbal one, in that it has its dialects, regional quirks and other devices akin to a verbal language. In its likeness to verbal linguistics, it can be learned as a second language and its various attributes can be picked up, committed to memory and imitated.

Something that needs to be expanded on is the idea of chivalry when it comes to dating. There is an outmoded notion that if you are 'chivalrous' to someone then they somehow owe you something. This tends to come from people who talk about 'the friend zone'. The point is, when it comes to males and females, girls do often get more attention than guys, but not all attention is good attention! It makes it more difficult to actually find someone suitable – I've had a lot of friends who are girls who guys have tried to use just for sex. The biggest piece of advice I can give is to treat people equally. If you're going on a date with a girl, even if you pay for things, they do not owe you anything. In turn, if you're going on a date with a guy and you're a girl, the guy is in no way obliged to pay for things. When I go on a date with a girl, what I usually do is get the bill and just say, 'I'll get this one, and you can pay for it next time.' That way you're letting the girl know that you're both on an even footing and it'll be appreciated. Girls are not vending machines – you don't put kindness in to get sex out. If this is in any way whatsoever your thinking, get out of it. You'll get a lot more out of life that way.

BIG DUMB SEX

Let me first broach this difficult subject with a simple sentiment, an 'ice breaker', if you will. It is this: sex is great. Seriously, good, bad, it's all life affirming and carries with it one of those fantastic juxtapositions where even though everyone is doing it, it's still an incredibly taboo subject; and I mean literally everyone of age is doing it. I hate to say it, but it is the reason you exist, and continues to be a lot of people's *raison d'être* later on in life. It's still a mystery to me why it's as off-limits in conversational canon as it is. The mere mention of it is enough to send people into fits of giggles or outrage and at the very least make them blush. The problem with this subject being taboo is that the stigma attached is self-perpetuating. People fear the unknown, and by way of reproach, it is pushed further into the realm of the unknown, in a kind of self-sustaining loop.

The key, however, as with a lot of things, is communication, and this applies throughout the whole process. I think the best way to start would be at the beginning, and I'll do my best to talk through the process. First and foremost, and most important, is consent. To put it simply, and in a way that will be obvious to anyone, no means no. While it is a difficult subject, often the main premise of rape is one of a kind of 'begrudging desire', the idea that even though someone flat out refuses, often even physically, they somehow actually mean yes. I know this isn't something that really needs to be said here, but often there is a culture of bravado and some people's advice can be unhelpful. Consent is still a hotly contested topic, and in my opinion it shouldn't be. The point is, if there is any doubt whatsoever as to whether or not the person is consenting, or whether or not the person is in the right frame of mind to consent, then you shouldn't go ahead with anything. Alongside this, if the person consents in the first place and then changes their mind, they are completely okay to do so.

There was a great metaphor I saw recently about consent, which likened sex to a cup of tea. If you offer someone a cup of tea, i.e. sex, and they refuse, that's okay. If you offer someone a cup of tea and they can't say yes or no, you still don't pour tea down their neck. If they want tea and then halfway through decide they don't want it, then sure, you've boiled the kettle and all, but sometimes they just don't feel like the tea. If they say yes but they're so drunk they're incapable of drinking tea, then of course you shouldn't just make them drink it – you make sure they're okay and let it go. If there's ever any doubt whether or not they want tea, you never try to push tea on them, because sometimes they just don't want a cup of tea. This is probably both the most potent and the most English way of looking at consent I've ever seen, but it's definitely one to take notice of. (NB: This is just an analogy – sex has nothing to do with tea. Unless you're into that kind of thing.)

A lot of advice on the subject of sex is unhelpful at best, and the reason for this is simply based around segregation. There is a culture of separation, propagated by a widening awareness of Asperger's. With awareness doesn't always come understanding, and this is a problem. While I don't mean to get too picky on the subject, what I'm trying to say is that there needs to be less talk of 'people with Asperger's', and more recognition of people on the autism spectrum as people, with Asperger's. When people talk about Asperger's and sexuality, or indeed other subjects, I often hear 'people with AS do this' or 'people with AS don't do that'. People with AS are people, have their own likes, dislikes, quirks, strengths and weaknesses. We are all human and if every AS person was the same we'd be pretty boring.

The reason why there is so much unhelpful advice, or rather, a lack of any decent advice when it comes to talking about sex and ASD, seems to go much deeper than anything to do with the autism spectrum – it pertains to social convention itself. On researching the topic when it came to writing this chapter, I found that most guides tended to skip straight from menstruation and puberty to relationships, with maybe a brief nod to sexual relationships somewhere in between. I hope you'll pardon my language when I say that the problem, both when it comes to the autism spectrum and sexuality in general, is that everything is so fucking *figurative*. I left sex education trying to figure out how a penis could be a banana, and the vagina a diagram. Everything is so steeped in metaphor that it becomes difficult to work out what's real and what's not, and all the while there is only talk of biology without any mention of sexual convention. I'm sick of 'sexual behaviour' and 'sexual relationships'. Sometimes it's not well behaved, and the two people aren't in a relationship. Society has become scared of the word 'sex' and it's become a stumbling block to better sex education for those with and without an ASD.

Sex can be a minefield for people with Asperger's Syndrome, as there are any number of problems that can occur: an inability to deal with the multitude of emotions that surround it, sensory issues that can be involved and the social rules that exist. I have never struggled with sex, so much as with the intimacy that surrounds it, and much of this is grounded in the sensory experiences that come with it. This is where good communication comes into play, as often this can be solved simply by talking with your partner to try to come up with some compromise. For example, soft physical contact for me, at times, is almost unbearable. Someone affectionately stroking my arm or my face can feel as if they're digging for oil in the same spot. It's physically painful, a strong burning sensation. However, when pressure is applied, the sensation is pleasant. It seems a little backward, but unfortunately that's just the way it is. When it comes to sexuality and autism, frank communication and the compromise that accompanies it are key to a good sex life, as sex can be fraught with sensory difficulties, and these need to be worked through in a way that is best for both parties.

For me, sex in a relationship has been great, but it has been incredibly stressful too. Working out when sex is a good idea, in what situations, when it's not a good idea, like after an argument – all these little nuances – is impossibly difficult. Then there is avoiding advances from other people, and recognising when these people are making sexual advances. Saying no is difficult when you don't understand what's happening in the first place. Sex itself isn't the problem. Like a lot of people with Asperger's, when I broach an entirely new subject with a whole new world of possibilities (and possibilities for error), *I research.* I looked up everything. However, while I know about sex, and I am good at it, it became (and still is to some extent) a huge stumbling block. Sex seemed simple and carnal – it was a respite from the terrifying cacophony of human emotion that was the outside world. However, this became a problem in relationships because this dissociation of sex from emotion was almost a way of avoiding difficult topics. It became a way to cope, and at one point almost became an addiction. It came to be a respite not only from AS but from bipolar too, as it seemed to be the only thing that 'levelled me out'. However, the respite was only brief with respect to both disorders – it was a fleeting way to gain control.

I was lucky growing up in that I do not come from a conservative family – we were open and honest about sex, and so I have no qualms in talking about it. In particular, sexuality was never an issue in our family, though the idea of homophobia was a talking point – it was always difficult to understand since our ideas tend to be based around reason and logic. There are studies that suggest a higher rate of homosexuality when it comes to autism and I think that may be because people on the spectrum are more pragmatic when it comes to personal relationships.

My and my family's attitudes to sex have always been open, but this was never going to be literary pornography, otherwise this would be an altogether difficult book. It's not that kind of user guide, and I think I'd get into trouble with the publisher using those kind of illustrations. The thing is, attitudes to sexuality within the autism spectrum often tend to be almost bipolar. Sex isn't all talk; it's tactile and action-based, so with certain people, especially within a relationship, it can seem like a means to establish a connection with someone and express feelings in a way that transcends the communicational stumbling blocks of autism. For many others, the exact opposite is true; sex can be so confusing, so sensitive to the slightest difference of touch and opinion, and is so varied from person to person, that it is often avoided altogether. While I am in no way saying there are only these two polar opposites when it comes to autism and sexuality, there is a recurring theme and within the autism spectrum asexuality is more common than it is in the general population.

There are a number of ethical factors to bear in mind when it comes to sexual etiquette, and people should consider these whether they are on the autism spectrum or not. Things like cat-calling in the street should have been confined already to a less civilised past. Such things are still part of sexual behaviour and they work on the premise of sexualising people without their consent. In general, simply asking people for sex when you've first met them isn't a good idea – it debases them as a person and makes you come across as shallow. Basically, you're disregarding their personality and reducing them to a sexual object. Other ways of being polite are more ensconced in the act of sex – things like pleasuring the other person during sex. Sex is a shared act, so be considerate to the other person's feelings. This is where sex education falls short; biology is talked about in depth, but it's cold and clinical. From there, young people try to bridge the knowledge gap through pornography and adult films, but this is an inadequate medium for learning about sexual etiquette as it is full of overplay, acting and unrealistic scenarios and lacks the 'after the fact' scenario of sex. There is a hell of a lot more than just penetration when it comes to sex.

Sex is messy, whichever way you paint it, and a lot of people on the autism spectrum struggle to cope with that level of mess. If people on the spectrum learn from unrealistic portrayals of sex, such as pornography, then the problem is compounded. Sex education doesn't teach you that you should keep a towel handy, or that sometimes people make weird noises during sex, or that there are way more fluids than you expect. It's pretty understandable that a lot of people on the autism spectrum may become disillusioned or disenfranchised with sex and become asexual through choice, a way to bow out of a confusing and strange world. There seem to be so many different rules and ways to act in terms of sexuality that nobody is told and we just have to learn.

On the other hand, however, the human body varies so wildly and wonderfully from person to person, and this is a great thing. Everybody acts differently, feels things completely differently, and likes different things. Learning this is something of an adventure, and as someone on the autism spectrum, it gives me comfort that whatever my sensory difficulties and sensitivities are, I am in no way broken, just different. Sensory difficulties do make a difference, too. When it comes to sex, there is a constant search for common ground and compromise in terms of coping with sensory sensitivities. Every smell can be magnified, every sound heightened, every touch almost climactic. Dealing with each sense is difficult, but there are certain ways I use to cope with each one separately.

- **Sound:** Certain sounds can be piercing, and others can be just a little repulsive. Often, with individuals on the autism spectrum, the threshold for people's intolerance to certain sounds is lowered. The aversion can be to do with volume, but sometimes sounds with certain 'aural textures' can cause repulsion. Sounds like squelching, or two materials such as rubber rubbing together are like nails on a chalkboard – nigh on intolerable. You don't need to have the most vivid imagination to work out that when it comes to sex, this could cause problems. The way I overcame this personally was by masking out those particular sounds or dulling them by playing music at the same time. It sounds like a cliché, but carrying around music and a speaker, since the age of inexpensive mobile phones, is becoming easier and easier. This doesn't mask the sounds completely (unless you're wearing earphones, which I'd advise against as it is kind of a moment-killer) but it does dull them to an acceptable level. If you do want to block out the sounds completely, then ear-plugs can be a good idea. It seems strange, but there are ones you can buy that are completely unnoticeable. Do remember that these cut off all noise (except more expensive ones, which cut off noise of a certain frequency) so this does rule out certain sexual activities. Talking dirty isn't that great when you can't hear a thing!

- **Smell:** This was a big one for me; there are so many scents when it comes to sex and they can be overwhelming. They mix into a cacophony of various sensations that can completely overpower any sense of mood or concentration. For the sake of explanation, I'm going to split these into different types of smells, and the way to deal with the negative aspects of each:

‣ Ambient smells – the general 'sex smell' and the smells within the room itself, such as food, paper, books and laundry. Air freshener is the way forward here – some are better than others, and it's good to work out which you prefer beforehand. Otherwise, incense or candles work wonders, incense more so, as there's less chance of setting the place on fire.

‣ Localised smells – foot or body odour (it sounds grim, but often sex has no sense of timing – it can be after a romantic date or after a heavy day at work), deodorant, aftershave or perfume, or genitals (different people smell different down there – this is an entirely natural thing, and in general it isn't in any way unpleasant). Often in this situation, if a smell is offensive, I find that bluntness helps more than anything – just make light of the situation. Say you can smell how hard they've been working. Be assertive, say it with a smile and make a joke of it. There are subtler ways to go about it; in a relationship, shower sex is great, but don't make it a routine though. Otherwise, take antiperspirant around with you, use it and then offer it to your partner. This serves a double purpose, because generally it is followed by the question, 'Why, do I smell?' to which you can answer, 'A little at the moment, maybe!' By not being too serious about it and adding 'at the moment' you are highlighting the point that this is just a transient state and they don't smell in general. There's a fine line between being honest and dampening someone's confidence.

› I'm going to note one last thing – I'm unsure whether other people experience this, but to me people have their own scent, which varies from person to person. It is a unique identifier and isn't generally unpleasant, but it can become overpowering. Generally, it's a mix of perfume or aftershave, deodorant and cosmetic products – try to work out which one is offensive, explain about the sensory side of things and just be completely honest. Don't overplay it – be confident that this is how you are, and don't feel embarrassed or apologetic about it.

- **Touch:** Hypersensitivity to touch in a sexual environment is easily the most difficult of the senses to manage. Touch in terms of sexuality can be almost cacophonous, a myriad of different textures, temperatures and pressures that can be difficult to cope with. For me, it isn't so much the various types of touch but the crossovers between them and the mix-ups that causes. The softest touch can be painful, and deep pressure pleasurable. While the first one tends to apply to those with sensory sensitivities, the second is common to those on the autism spectrum. Get to know your body and what feels right. Communication is key – let your partner know what feels good and what doesn't. 'Touch' extends past simply touching between you and your partner – be proactive in things like choosing bedsheets or moving around current ones. Obviously, during spontaneous sexual encounters, at someone else's house for example, you may not have as much control over whether you can change or move things like bedsheets and other aspects of your environment, but if something like that is bothering you, try to move it out of the way completely.

- **Taste:** You might not think at first the sensation of taste is something that applies to sex, but it does. We taste a lot in general before, during and after intercourse. Kissing. Fellatio. Cunnilingus. This side of sex is something that has only really been brought to the fore in recent years because it's very hard to be euphemistic when you really get into the dynamics of sex. Gustatory perception in sex is pretty all-pervasive – in general, lip-to-lip contact is a big part of sexuality, as is the touch of lips to skin. Whether someone has eaten, what they've eaten, whether they smoke, what they drink, all affects the way someone tastes. In terms of lip to skin contact, things like aftershave or perfume and shower gel, all play a part, too. When it comes to kissing, it's tough to subtly point out when a person's breath smells. Water helps; keep some cordial by the bedside to take the edge off. Offering chewing gum or a mint works, if you have one yourself, but make sure this is before the act! Chewing gum during sex is not attractive. In terms of ejaculate, the jury is out as to whether people can make it taste better. What is true, however, is that ejaculate is composed partly of glucose and fructose, so some people postulate that vegetables and fruit juice hours before sex can make it taste better. Otherwise, sucking a mint beforehand apparently helps, and has the side-effect of the added stimulation mint provides.

- **Sight:** In terms of a sexual environment (I'm not going to say a bedroom environment, as that suggests a lack of imagination), sight is a difficult one. Lighting is very important – full overhead lights can often add to anxiety and make the situation almost interrogatory. Keep to soft lights and lamps. This also avoids anything too bright. As those on the autism spectrum often focus on details, make sure not to keep your attention narrowed to one part of the body.

Communication is key when it comes to sex. Don't be afraid to be sexually assertive – that means vocalising what feels good and what you like. Never push, however; if someone doesn't want to do something, you should never try to coerce them into it. Sex is great, and a decent rapport and honesty are the key ingredients to make it work. Respect your partner, have confidence in yourself and have fun!

RELATIONSHIPS AND ASPERGER'S

I've been pontificating over what to write in terms of this chapter for some time and a friend pointed out that maybe that, in itself, is something to write about. I've started writing sections of this about three times, possibly in various states of melancholy when it comes to relationships, and I can't help but think I may be in over my head here. I've had a range of relationships, some lasting weeks, others lasting years, but if there's one thing I do know it's that I'm still learning – I think we're all still learning. I'm in no way an expert and part of the reason this chapter is so difficult is because of that fact – I feel like a fraud. The thing is, relationships are difficult. They are a veritable minefield of miscommunication, misinterpretation, misunderstanding (and, apparently, alliteration).

Relationships can be hard, but they can also be incredibly rewarding, can lighten the tough times, and that electric feeling you get when you're with your 'other half' can actually make you believe there is some truth in that expression. You feel like two halves of a whole. Sometimes (and I am a firm believer, through no belief in fate or some higher power, but through sheer probability, that this happens to everyone who has contact with people at some point) you just 'connect' with someone. You care about what happens to them, you think about them when they aren't there. You're on the same 'wavelength'. Think of two sounds played that harmonise with each other, whose waveforms complement each other – this expression makes more sense than most. You might even find yourselves finishing each other's sentences. (I hope one day to find someone who does this with my writing, as it would make writing these books a lot easier!)

The crux of my ramblings is this – relationships are hard work, but they can be worth it. The next chapter should detail, at least in some small way, how to play on the good points and overcome the bad. The key to living with Asperger's

Syndrome, even the key to living in general, is to identify your weaknesses, find some way to overcome them and turn them into strengths – and making relationships work is no different. I speak from experience – some good, and some bad – but it's all helped me understand the world a little better. Whether positive, or negative, our experiences shape us, and when we spend whole years of our lives alongside another person, we pick up a lot along the way.

This chapter works heavily on the basis of 'do as I say, not as I do'. I'm no Lothario, no Casanova, and I am certainly no guru in this subject. This chapter is a conglomerate of information, an edit together of a multitude of information gleaned from a number of different people. These people include, well, pretty much everybody – family, friends, friends of family, family of friends, I'm sure you get the idea. It's important to remember, however, that much of a relationship goes on behind closed doors (no, I don't mean that part – get your mind out of the gutter!). So maybe it's just the cynic in me talking, but that perfect couple everyone knows and aspires to be, probably isn't so perfect at all.

I'll be frank here. This is a painful subject to write about – a while ago I came out of a two-and-a-half-year relationship with a girl I firmly believed I was going to grow old with. When the relationship ended, I was lost, and there was a long while where I was left all but broken. I didn't know how to act anymore, how to be myself. Recovering from that took a long time, longer than it should have, to be honest. I spent a lot of time trying to forget, or distract myself from her and the time we spent together, which is entirely unlike me and completely illogical. Human cognition doesn't work that way, we can't simply forget things at will, much as we'd like to. When you spend an extended period of time in a relationship with someone, you can't simply put them out of your mind. Forgetting them is tantamount to forgetting entire months or years of your life, and other than rare circumstances involving drugs or head trauma, humans don't tend to do this. It took far too long to realise that.

If forgetting isn't an option, then where do we go from there? People on the autism spectrum often have a tendency to fixate on certain things and commit them to memory more than other people. Non-spectrum people do this anyway within relationships, so when it comes to Asperger's Syndrome and the autism spectrum this works doubly so. In this sense, it's even more difficult to simply push things to the side. Even though at first I did try. Subsequently, *her* name was off-limits to anyone around me and any time she was mentioned it was enough to send my thoughts spiralling downwards. After a time I realised this simply wasn't the way to go and I did think about her. I thought about the time we'd spent together and what that meant to me. It was tough, but I learned to live with the memory of the times we had as opposed to disregarding or ignoring them.

During my later teenage years, Asperger's Syndrome seemed like a huge stumbling block to dealing with being in a relationship. For starters, I found the transition from 'dating' to being 'in a relationship' was something that often happened without my even knowing it. A lot of the time there wasn't any bridge between the two, and it was just something that I only found out when I was referred to as a 'boyfriend'. Sometimes, this was before the subject of Asperger's Syndrome and the autism spectrum had been broached, and a lot of the difficulties with communication and interaction I had – and still do have – at that point were still taken as idiosyncrasies. The tough part was that as the relationship progressed, the quirks were often ruled out as idiosyncrasy and perceived instead as full-on idiocy.

A few harsh lessons were learned back then. In particular, I found that running an emulator, that skill that had become so integral to 'pretending to be normal', was something that, in a relationship, just broke down. When you are with someone for extended periods of time, and when that person is someone invested in you enough to want to get to know all of your qualities, quirks and habits, they become pretty good at knowing when you're 'faking it'. I also found that communication is absolutely key when it comes to relationships – being open is crucial. In a relationship, everything is magnified, both your qualities and your shortcomings. In terms of communication, this means that there is no hiding your 'autism-isms'. When it comes to disclosure, it's important to be clear early in the relationship. As I've mentioned previously, don't keep bringing it up, however, as it breeds resentment and can seem as if you're making excuses.

One of the most important things in a relationship is honesty, not just with your partner, but with yourself. That means being honest with yourself if you feel you are changing in ways you don't like, or if you feel that you're not coping. Your health and your mental health are not worth sacrificing for your partner and you need to keep that in mind throughout the bad times. That said, I don't mean that you need to jump ship at the first sign of a problem; it's just that if you feel that your relationship is contributing to or causing any mental health issues, it may be time to take a break.

Thus far I've painted the world of dating and relationships as, at the very least, convoluted and, at its worst, a bit of a pain in the ass. So how do we make sense of this strange world? Bulleted lists, of course. Here are some tips on surviving in a relationship:

- First off, you are both only human and so you need to allow for that! Your autism spectrum disorder doesn't make your way of thinking in any way superior to someone without a diagnosis, in the same way as a person on the spectrum isn't in any way inferior. Get any ideas of a 'them' and 'us' out of your head when it comes to autism, and put you and you partner on a level playing field – in a relationship, you're both equals. Your various foibles and qualities are just different – some of them may be down to autism, some may just be personal quirks.

- When it comes to advice, don't take anything as gospel, and don't constantly live according to other people's word. Take every piece of advice you are given with a pinch of salt. (Even this! Well, kind of.) Following advice to the letter is one of the worst things you can do. When you start to follow a script, life becomes dull and boring. You'll be constantly working out what to say and do next and there's a good chance you'll come across as robotic and disinterested. When it comes to relationship advice, use it as guidelines or suggestions rather than rules to follow to the letter. You know your partner better than the writer of some internet article.

- Play to your strengths and use them to work on your weaknesses. I often find it difficult to talk about emotions in the conventional way, and in a relationship this leads to problems. Writing has long been a passion of mine, so now I use SMS and social media chat to say how I feel instead. I don't do this often, but it does help.

- Compromise with your interests; make sure you share in your partner's interests as well as yours, and get them to join in with yours (if they want to!). If you have a specialist subject, and your partner takes an interest, make sure you appreciate that and repay them in turn by investing in their passions.

- Be open and up front with any issues you might have sooner rather than later. That means sitting down and talking through things that you might struggle with, like needing space or needing to take five minutes out now and again when social situations get too difficult. If these things become the norm early on, it is much easier to assimilate them into the relationship.

- Don't just shut off when things get tough! Some people on the autism spectrum have a tendency to internalise things and this simply isn't good. If you keep your feelings in and bottle them up, eventually something will have to give and there's a good chance that if you've been harbouring negative feelings in a relationship for a while, it will be explosive. If you're having problems in some way, talk to your partner about it. Broach the subject gently, if it's about them, but still make the effort to communicate – it will be appreciated.

- In the opposite sense, make sure you don't lash out either. When you get angry and frustrated, it can be easy to externalise issues and take it out on someone else, and when that someone else is your partner it can put a strain on the relationship. Talk frankly to your partner about any issues and if you can find a vent, do, whether it's music, arts, fitness, friends or whatever your specialist subject may be.

- Some advice for partners of those on the spectrum: Be aware that outside influences will affect someone with an ASD much more and so it's important when changes in behaviour or problems present themselves to look at things situationally rather than emotionally. Look at external stimuli; if someone on the spectrum seems distracted or distant, often they won't know how they are feeling in the first place so pushing the issue is just going to cause more stress. If you can, try to deal with the external stimuli rather than the feelings they produce, as getting to the root of the problem yields much better results.

When someone acts 'normal' outside a relationship, it can be easy for a partner to forget that someone is on the autism spectrum. This usually leads to a stark reminder in the form of some slight meltdown or mishap. The thing is, in relationships, Asperger's Syndrome and autism really aren't that easy to hide or suppress, so my suggestion is simply not to try. Be open and honest and you may find that the quirks and different ways of thinking that ASD present can really benefit the relationship and help keep a spark going that's often difficult to maintain in conventional relationships.

⑧
GROWING UP

AS WE MATURE, WE often hear people talk of growing up as an integral part of adulthood. The word has become something of a trope, a cliché even. It's used as an insult – we often say people need to 'grow up'. In the same sense, it can also be a compliment – it can be said that someone has grown up a lot, or that they're being very grown up when dealing with a particularly difficult situation in a mature manner. We often talk about people who lack maturity as 'still having a lot of growing up to do'. This isn't an insult in itself – it simply refers to the idea of naivety sometimes inherent in those who are younger and therefore can lack life experience. The process of growing up speaks of a rite of passage into adulthood and yet there is still a slight ambiguity that surrounds the subject as a whole.

When people talk about growing up, it generally means facing up to subjects you would otherwise shy away from.

This can pertain to a number of different things: it can be braving situations you otherwise wouldn't; it can be an act of selflessness or a personal sacrifice for the greater good; growing up can also be moving 'past the now' and planning for the future where you would usually just focus on the present; it can mean forgiving, making reconciliations with or simply just being civil to someone who has wronged you. The process of growing up doesn't mean that you don't struggle with these things, it just means that you push yourself past that initial struggle to better yourself or for the betterment of other people.

Personally, I imagined that I'd hit a certain age and be *all grown up*. I thought I'd get to 18 and suddenly lack enjoyment in certain areas. I had this idea that after a certain age I'd forgo my taste in rock and metal music for country and easy listening, that I'd relinquish my love of gigs in lieu of staying in with a glass of wine, or start talking about the good old days to anyone who would listen. In reality, it's more of a gradual process than that. I realised that letting things go was easier than it was when I was younger – I could be around people who had wronged me and still be civil so as not to cause tension, or for work reasons. I realised that I was starting to put money aside and think of the future – though a lot of it was in aid of my daughter, Alexis. These things didn't happen in a day; it was a gradual process that took some time. That said, there are times when everyone notices these things, and often times when people get scared about them.

A lot of people ruminate about growing up and I think part of this lies in its links to mortality. People often see maturity and mortality as bedfellows and can develop a Peter Pan complex based on a fear of becoming less able to do the things they enjoy. This is often unfounded; even though it can be more difficult to do certain things to the level that someone younger can, there are enough case studies to show that it is possible. (Though I must stress that I am 26 at the time of writing, and obviously being in the prime of my youth, I may not have yet felt the ravages of time creeping up on me!) Ironically, part of growing up is acknowledging that humans do age, and there are a few things that age you prematurely. Going out drinking every night and eating junk food all day may seem great at the time but you'll find that you start to see the physical repercussions before too long. (Also, poor nutrition and overconsumption of alcohol carry their own more short-term problems.)

A great signifier for growing up is the way we deal with our trials and tribulations, and this is where the path to 'adulthood' for those with ASD and those who aren't on the spectrum differs. In some respects, those on the autism spectrum can deal with various troubles better than some other people. By nature, those on the spectrum tend to be problem solvers and as such look for solutions to problems faced through action. In this sense, they can be more proactive than others in terms of growing up. When you have more to deal with on a day-to-day basis, it can mean that you learn to deal with day-to-day problems a little bit more quickly and a little bit more proficiently than people who don't have to face problems like anxiety and social faux pas. How you deal with this side of things denotes maturity, too. As I've grown older, I've learned a few tricks to deal with social faux pas and to brush off anxiety, garnered over time through experience.

Ironically, one of the greatest stepping stones on the way to maturity is being wrong. Not just being wrong per se – a lot of people of people do that, unfortunately. A great deal of maturity lies in recognising when you are wrong and dealing with it accordingly. A big part of growing up is the ability to apologise and to recognise your shortcomings. People make mistakes, and it's important to realise when you are doing so. You're human (and if you're not and you're reading this, then well done you) and to err is the most human of qualities. Don't begrudge yourself your foibles, simply recognise that life is a journey and that when walking the path you choose, you are bound to stumble a little along your way. On top of this, it's also important to recognise that others make mistakes too, and it is our erroneous nature that binds us together as a species. Next time you are wronged by someone, look at the nature of their misdeed. Was it an isolated incident? Is it conceivable that you could or may have done the same thing yourself? Try to switch places, however difficult that may be. Often it helps to relate to previous, similar and real situations that may have transpired in the past. While forgiving is difficult, it can be liberating letting go of a grudge – grudges, by their nature, take effort to maintain, especially if you're in contact with that person a great deal, so letting go of them can do wonders.

None of us is exempt from judgement, and this applies to people on or not on the spectrum. With everyone, there are factors to consider during the cognitive process we employ when we create a 'character map' of someone. When we look at someone on the autism spectrum, it's important to look at them in terms of their humanity alongside various aspects of the spectrum. That means realising that people with any autism spectrum disorder have good days, bad days, moody days, giddy days and days filled with every kind of human emotion, just like anyone not on the spectrum. In other words, in all likelihood they are capable of both the utmost graciousness and the most venomous spite, as are we all.

If you're on the spectrum and you're always struggling, keep in mind that everybody does, and that we all mess up sometimes, spectrum or not. We are none of us free from judgement, but I have seen people on the autism spectrum meet this teetering challenge of civility, diplomacy and emotional and moral intelligence better than some people not on the spectrum. Over time, I have watched people with autism grow to become something fantastic to behold and to show qualities that honestly make me proud to be on the spectrum.

HOW TO MAKE FRIENDS AND INFLUENCE PEOPLE

As you grow older, making friends ceases to become something that is simply beneficial and becomes something that can be actually needed to get ahead in life. However, the difference is that while as children we simply had our friends and our enemies, as adults we have entire tiers of friendship. The people we meet take on different roles. We have acquaintances, we have contacts and we have mentors. Each of these galvanise us as people, and each serve different roles. Differentiating between these roles is never easy and there are a lot of cross-overs between them, but they still exist. While keeping this in mind, there is still one thing that needs clarifying. This is that people are not there to be used, and while I have talked about different types of friends serving different 'purposes' I only mean in the way they are perceived, not how they should be used. A contact isn't someone whose sole role is to provide a service in their specialised field should it be needed, and a mentor isn't there solely to teach. On a personal level, I dislike the idea of categorising people as 'useful' or 'useless'. A hammer is useful, a screwdriver is useful, but to condense humanity, with all its grace and spite, into a mere tool, seems both over-simplistic and irresponsible.

But I digress. Before going into the nuances and subtleties of various *types* of friendship, it might be prudent to talk about making friends in the first place. I used to struggle a lot with making friends – the idea of speaking to somebody with absolutely no base for conversation was a concept that just seemed completely nonsensical. How do you talk to someone when you have absolutely nothing to talk to them about? The logic there is sound, but is still a little premature. In actual fact, when you first meet someone new, it's not that you have nothing to talk to them about, but that you have nothing to talk to them about *yet*. The conversation doesn't have to be mundane; it can be interesting, exciting even. When you meet a new person, you have so much to learn from them. You might find someone that you click with, and with whom you have a whole load of interests and pastimes in common. You share stories and sometimes they can change your entire perspective on life. Even when you meet someone with entirely conflicting values, or who you simply don't like, they can still change your way of thinking, and you can still learn from their actions and the consequences of them.

In the past, I had no idea how to make friends. This was partly because I was scared to approach people I didn't know and chat to them – I think there is an element of this in even the most extroverted of folk. However, I was always keen to move past this; there is both an inherent and inherited sense of stubbornness (thanks, Mum) that pushes me to challenge the things that scare me. The root of my difficulties lay in the fact that the dynamics of conversation (and at that point, body language) were still a mystery to me. Conversation would simply dry up and I'd have no idea why, especially when initially we seemed to be 'getting on'. There would be an awkward silence, and then an excuse would be made and the person I was talking to would take their leave. I had no idea why it would happen and how we could go from chatting comfortably to complete silence so quickly. At first, it was simply a point of annoyance, a slightly irritating side-effect of day-to-day sociality. After a time, however, it began to agitate me more and more; it became debilitating, something that hampered my everyday life and increasingly started to stunt personal relationships.

It was around this time that I had something of a conversational revelation, an epiphany of sociality, if you will.

Instead of viewing conversing as a subconscious process, as I had done before, I started to look at it as a craft, something to be shaped and nurtured. The more it was held under observation, the more nuances and subtleties it yielded and the more complex and fascinating it became. I started to look at not just the way people moved, gesticulated and held themselves, but the conversation itself. I observed the way people's conversation ebbed and flowed into something rhythmic and liquid, and the effect was entirely interesting, like watching a memory map played out in real time. What was curious was the way the conversation branched out and it was at that point the realisation struck me that the key lay in association and the fractal nature of conversation.

The concept of conversation as 'fractal', where one conversational topic branches out into others, is much simpler in theory than in practice. It still took (and takes) a lot of practice to get it right, but I started to improve my conversational skills when I realised that the way to keep a conversation going was to stick to a common theme throughout the conversation. Follow the subject of the conversation as it forms, then carry on by continuing a theme by incorporating or moving onto subjects relative to the first. A great way to both demonstrate this and practise conversational technique is through the 'word association game'. Take a word, then either by yourself or in a group, think of a word associated with that word in some way. Then, think of one associated with the last word. Give around a five-second time limit for each word and try to keep up the pace as much as you can. I used to use this game as practice to improve conversational technique a lot when I was younger and it definitely does help.

One of the more important things you should keep in mind is that your interests are yours and not necessarily those of the person you are talking to. Do listen to the person you are talking to. Really listen. There are times, such as when I have a reply already assembled in my head, I've found myself simply waiting for my turn to speak. It took a lot of self-awareness and honest self-reflection to get past that. Take in what they are saying and keep it in mind when you carry on the conversational thread. If the person's interests are the same as yours, great, but if the conversation has absolutely nothing to do with your specialist subject, then keep the talk away from it. I'm in no way saying steer away from that which interests you, but try to avoid giant, leaping tangents, as they tend to be conversation killers.

An interesting part of conversation and sociality which isn't touched on much is the way physical spaces affect conversation in a positive or negative way. This is massively important, especially in terms of making friends. We often don't get to choose the place we stage our first conversation in the process of making friends, as networking in general is something we often tend to do throughout our day-to-day lives. Obviously, how much we can choose the environment in which we socialise changes from person to person, between cultures and throughout different regions (think networking nights and business meetings, for example) but there will still be times where we will be thrown into situations where we are expected to mingle at a moment's notice.

Our attention and the way we converse changes depending on the space we occupy. In bigger spaces, bigger groups of people are prevalent, with more than one conversation happening, something I like to think of as 'multi-threading'. In smaller spaces, smaller groups are more common, with little space between people. Conversation tends to be more focused, and only one or two people speak at once in a group. The shape of a room focuses people's attention, too – think of a lecture theatre and how it uses the shape of the room to guide people's gaze to the lecturer. The idea of physicality affecting conversation transcends physical spaces and extends all the way to how people position themselves within a group. If you watch a group conversation for any length of time, you start to see that people position themselves in certain places almost instinctively when conversing and that groups of people tend to form a circle to better facilitate conversation. Watching the 'status' of this is important. If someone is unwelcome, they will often be closed out of the circle, cutting them off from the thread of discussion.

It would seem, reading through this chapter, that conversation is less of a pastime or an activity and more of a formulaic process, governed by a select set of social rules and stipulations. This is far from true; conversation is a craft and while there is a certain ethos that surrounds it and certain tips and tricks to get ahead, a lot of it is down to imagination and personal taste. There will be people you get on with like a house on fire, and people you simply don't 'click' with. Other times, you will click with people who you later struggle to converse with. Sociality in terms of discussion is fluid in nature, so it's important not to be disheartened when it comes to meeting new people. There are times when I've kicked myself for saying completely the wrong thing at the wrong moment, times when I've completely surprised myself and times when I've laughed at myself for saying something that legitimately pushes the boundaries of idiocy. Even though it feels deadly important at the time, take it in good humour. The only regrets I have aren't from things I've said, but things I haven't – there are many times when I could have made a friend but have been too scared of saying the wrong thing. It occurs less and less often as you grow older, but it still happens. More often than not, you regret what you don't say more than what you do.

Starting a conversation is always difficult. There are all kinds of techniques for 'breaking the ice' and hundreds, maybe even thousands, of conversational openers. If you want to try some of these out, go for it, but often the best thing to open with is a simple greeting. Even doing this can be immensely difficult, so spending time trying to think of some witty opener is often time better spent conversing. Part of the reason why a lot of conversational openers don't work is that the speaker is too focused on how they come across in a conversation without giving much thought to who they might be conversing with. On a personal level, this indicates to me someone who very much cares about how they are perceived, and that isn't necessarily a great thing. It's very difficult just to be yourself if you need constant affirmation that it's okay to do so. Be comfortable both with your strengths and your weaknesses and if you make mistakes, try to ensure they're your own, so you can properly learn from them.

Is there a way, then, to navigate this minefield of conversation unscathed? The short – and slightly daunting – answer is no. Becoming proficient in conversation is kind of a trial by fire – the chances are, unless you get very, very lucky, you're going to make a lot of mistakes. Every mistake is useful, however. Try to take something from every discussion you have, whether creative and deep, or mundane and banal. Even though the art of conversation varies wildly from person to person (and therein lies its beauty) there are a few topics that tend to resonate with people as a whole, and some that tend to make conversation turn sour.

GO-TO TOPICS

- **Music and art:** I put these two together because the two cross paths fairly often, but in general people will have had some pretty positive experiences with one or the other. Be open in your views and remember some people may have different opinions to yours so the chances are, especially with music, you'll have a few shockers thrown your way. Don't be shy in confessing any guilty pleasures you may have in terms of both music and art.

- **Fun:** This is such a wide and varied topic, and opens up the thread of conversation to a million and one different anecdotes. You can get some great stories from asking people what their favourite pastimes are and what they like to do for fun. People are generally passionate about their recreation and so by bringing up this conversational topic you are sowing the seed for entire threads of conversation.

- **Food:** People's eating habits vary wildly from person to person. There are some who live to eat and some who simply eat to live, and everything in between. It's a good topic to talk about, but can lead to conversational 'blanks' when someone just really isn't all that interested in food. People tend to be passionate about food that ties into certain cultures, and so this also works as a decent segue into other topics.

- **People:** This sounds like an odd one, but people are always a good source of conversation. There are a few different sides to this: Mutual friends are a good topic of conversation, if you have them. In particular, if you have friends in the arts or music scene, you can talk about that. Otherwise, stories about other people and interesting anecdotes you've been told by friends can take the conversation away from you, which is good. You can very easily come across as self-absorbed when you only have yourself to relate to.

- **Aspirations:** This one is huge and a little scary, but wonderful in that respect. As you grow older, the kid question, 'What do you want to be when you grow up?' matures with you, but still remains. What are the hopes and dreams of the person you're talking to and how do they match yours? Aspirations and ambitions is a topic that has many different levels to it and I've found it's often better to let the other person decide how to answer that question and how much depth to go into. When I meet someone new, I usually ask, 'What do you do, what are your passions?' That way, they can give as much or as little depth to their answer as they want, without feeling pressured.

- **Surroundings:** Conversationally, this is a difficult one, because when done wrong it can be a complete cliché and you can stumble headlong into the realm of the tedious. This tends to work as a 'filler' or a discussion-based primer, used to fill in the blanks when there is a lull in conversation. The British are pro at it – just think how often we talk about the weather. That said, when you're bombarded by four seasons in one day, talking about the weather (possibly while dodging hailstones and squinting through the blinding snow or dazzling sunshine) becomes a little easier.

- **Current events:** By current events, I don't mean what's happening right in your field of vision, but rather the opposite. What's going on outside your sphere of influence, what's happening overseas? Sometimes we get so wrapped up in our own lives, we forget that there is a big wide world out there and there's a lot going on in it. This doesn't automatically mean you're selfish or self-centered, just that you have a life to lead, and that often you encounter problems within that. Even though our problems often pale in comparison to those of other people, they still trouble us on a personal level. When you widen your attention to things happening in the next city, across the border, overseas, around the world and into all social and ethnic groups, you don't just broaden your knowledge of current events, but your cultural knowledge too and your conversational scope. Humanity is capable of the most wonderful feats. Talk about them, get enthused about them, get passionate, and then pass that on. This sentiment transcends mere conversation – the more you extend your attention outside your immediate vicinity, the more you start to put a little perspective on your own trials and tribulations.

NO-GO TOPICS

- **Finances:** There are some people who will talk about their finances with reckless abandon and these are generally the type of people who don't need to worry about them. For other people, finances are a source of worry and sometimes even panic. It doesn't matter whether you're feeling flush or if you're strapped for cash, talking about money can cause people to judge you prematurely and those judgements are not always positive. Besides that, if you've had a windfall recently and you talk about it, not-so-kind people may latch onto that and see you as someone to use. This can be either directly in terms of a source of monetary income, where you'll find a 'new friend' asking to borrow money, or as someone who will be available to party at a moment's notice. If you're strapped for cash and you talk about it at great length, people can take it as hinting at a request to borrow money and that, in a new friend, isn't a great quality.

- **Work:** There are two sides to the argument about work as a conversational 'no-go'. I herald it as an 'invitation-only' kind of topic for discussion. The thing is, there are people who like their job, even love it. I'm one of those people, but I'm also very aware that there are also people who dislike or hate their jobs, and when the topic is brought up it brings up all the emotions that are attached to that. More often than either of these, you will find people who lie somewhere in between love and hate in terms of work. For a lot of people, work is work – you can like your job, but still not want to talk about it constantly. I tend to talk about work briefly on meeting someone in a day-to-day environment, for example introductions in a café or coffee shop, but steer away from it in terms of more recreational activities. The reasoning behind this lies in the fact that, generally, people don't want to think about work when they're having time away from it. Work time is work time, and playtime is playtime.

- **Insecurities:** Conversation, at least to a certain point, should be constructive. When it comes to insecurities, this definitely isn't the case. Talking about something brings it to the forefront of your mind. When meeting new people, bringing negative thoughts to the front of your mind and into the conversation isn't a great idea. It can show the cracks in your confidence and serve to highlight flaws that sometimes aren't even there. If you feel you do something a little differently or oddly, don't highlight that as a negative factor on first meeting someone. In externalising your issues, you cement them in someone's mind as something negative before they have a chance to make up their mind themselves.

- **Misanthropy**: There are really no good points to this as a conversational topic. When two people dislike a certain person, sometimes it can become a bonding subject and can bring them closer. However, if you've shunned humanity and are nurturing a low-level hatred for the human condition, there are very few people who are going to want to talk at length about just that on meeting you. There are a couple of key factors to misanthropy: one is that it generalises an entire species, and the other is that it causes one to have a fairly negative outlook on the world. By generalising so wildly when you first meet someone, it gives the impression that you aren't going to appreciate them entirely for who they are. The negative outlook comes from the fact that because people are so interwoven into the structure of the planet we inhabit, if you harbour a disdain or dislike for people then that will taint all areas of life.

DIVISIVE TOPICS

On reading this you may be wondering what exactly constitutes a 'divisive topic', and I'd love to give an entirely clear answer to this, but I'm not altogether sure there is one. Divisive topics, as I see them, are binary topics – topics where there is no chance of middle ground. Politics in the UK is a great example – generally people are either left wing or right wing, and very few people rest neutrally in between those two schools of thought. If two people agree, this is fine, but when you have completely contrary opinions on something pivotal it can kill a friendship before you get to know that person's merits and can look past their opinions on certain subjects.

Keeping friends is something that in the past I often struggled with and it can serve as a yardstick for maturity. There are a few elements which are integral to keeping a friendship intact, including but not restricted to understanding, forgiveness and patience.

- Understanding in a friendship is important. As people become adults, they generally become busier and less available. Sometimes, especially if someone has a particularly hectic lifestyle, you may go for long periods without seeing a friend. Remember that alongside any other commitments they have, they will also have to divide their time among other friends too. A good friend won't begrudge the fact that someone is often too busy to spend time with them, but will be able to pick up from where they left off, even if the time between meetings is months or even years. Don't be too quick to judge when someone cancels on a meeting.

- Forgiveness is pretty key to maintaining a friendship. Nobody is perfect, and there are probably going to be times when you fall out with friends, for reasons that are either your fault, theirs, both or neither. Part of maintaining a long-lasting friendship is knowing when to apologise and when to accept an apology. There are even times when it's best to just let go of a disagreement for the sake of the friendship and chalk it down to a bad day. Obviously this takes a little judgement and it's important to be resolute in your opinions, but the old adage 'to err is human, to forgive divine' still often rings true. Falling out with someone doesn't automatically de-categorise them as a friend – almost everybody argues at some point in their lives.

- Patience is an important factor in any relationship, not just friendship. Often when people are going through difficult times, they just need you to be there to ride out the worst part, and to remind them that even the most tempestuous of storms eventually pass. Friendships can be difficult to maintain when your mind is on other things, and recognising that is crucial to upholding a friendship when times get tough.

I hope this chapter will prove to be of some use, but I cannot stress enough how important it is to regard each person as a separate entity. In any conversation there is a degree of adaptability that's required and part of the reasoning behind that is simply down to the wonderfully different and liquid nature of the human persona. Appreciate each person and become invested in them and their conversation. There is a fantastic quote by Dale Carnegie, American writer and lecturer on self-improvement, that has rung true on a personal level for a while now. It states that 'You can make more friends in two months by becoming really interested in other people than you can in two years by trying to get other people interested in you.' This is one of the most insightful truths in terms of meeting new people. Put away any misanthropy you may have, or any expectations you may have, and really *listen to* and take in what the other parties are saying. You may find that once you become interested, really interested, in what people have to say, they will start to appreciate that quality and become interested in you too.

ONWARDS TO ADULTHOOD

So you're an adult now – welcome to your new life of ups and downs. Now, before you curl up into the foetal position and hope it wears off, or go and search for Neverland on Google Maps, take a second. There are some great points to being an adult. Fair enough, you've got things like paperwork, responsibility and remembering to put the bins out, but you also have more independence and the opportunity for maturity and freedom of thought. When you're an adult, you're treated as such, and this is liberating, heady even. You spend your whole teenage life striving to be treated like an adult and then suddenly you grow past a certain age, and you are. Often, you're not even sure you're ready for it. The question is, where does this leave you if you have Asperger's Syndrome?

A lot of people are of the opinion that autism spectrum disorders somehow peter out, or that you somehow 'grow out' of them. I still hear comments about people who 'used to have Asperger's'. Asperger's Syndrome is liquid and changing in nature; it is susceptible to so many things in life, including stress and other external factors. There are situations where you may look and feel more 'normal' than other times, but it never fully goes away. As we become adults, we start to become better at running an emulator, and other people can forget that someone with Asperger's is different at all. These times are great; I'm happy with the change in perspective that AS gives me, but it is nice to have these 'breaks' where I can play at being off the spectrum for a little while. The problem is that this respite can only go on so long before reality comes knocking, and the reality is that being on the autism spectrum can be really, really hard.

Part of the difficulty of living on the spectrum in the adult world lies in the fact that autism and Asperger's Syndrome are still so-called 'invisible disabilities'. This fuzzy logic lies in the assumption that if the problems aren't physical, they must be not as severe, absent or just a product of a nanny state. This assumption extends way past the autism spectrum and all the way into mental health, where topics like depression, bipolar disorder and schizophrenia still don't get the credence they deserve, yet still bear all the stigma they have suffered in past years. Certain people have campaigned for both mental health and autism awareness in recent years, and their work is as important now as it ever was. That said, awareness of the existence of something isn't necessarily tantamount to awareness of the specifics behind it, and it certainly doesn't equal acceptance of the problems that surround it. There's still a certain amount of intolerance underlying both mental health and the autism spectrum.

The spectrum of autism is wide and varied and some people on the spectrum will be able to do things that other people will struggle with, and those same people may find something easy that others struggle with. When it comes to adulthood, it's not always easy to spot when someone is struggling, as often the people who struggle just get better at hiding it. Don't fret though, it's not all doom and gloom. As you grow older, you can develop ways of coping with situations better, and often you can stem a meltdown before it happens. On top of this, you generally have a little more freedom to do as you please; if you need to take five minutes out, you can do so. There are certain situations, like within employment, where you need to okay it with your employer first, but in general you can still do what's necessary to cope with the fast pace of adult life and come through the other side largely unscathed. On getting to this point, you'll have made a lot of social mistakes – don't worry too much about them, or at the very least learn from them. They've brought you to where you are now. I still, to this day, look back on some of my past social faux pas and cringe. However, in the past, it was with shame and, if I'm honest, something akin to self-hatred. There was a time when I ached to be 'normal', even just for a little bit, and each mistake, each meltdown, each tangential or inappropriate comment, each attack of anxiety highlighted how far I was away from that. Now, I look back with a mixture of nostalgia, slight amusement and a little pride that I've come as far as I have. I made mistakes – everybody does – but I learned from them and came through the other side a better person for it.

Living with Asperger's Syndrome and autism in the adult world involves learning to move past people's lack of acceptance. When I was younger, I was bullied so much, by so many people, that I never really knew what it was like to be around people who accepted me for me, who took my idiosyncrasies as quirks and accepted my flaws. On growing up, I realised that to move on, I was going to have to shrug off the opinions of a lot of people. You're not going to be able to please everyone, and so on growing up you have to realise you will wear things, like things, and do things that some people don't like, and some of those things will be tied into Asperger's Syndrome. You need to be strong and realise that some people won't accept that – those who are happiest often have a thick skin to match. When you find people who accept you for who you are, make sure you extend the same courtesy! As long as the opinions and quirks don't involve discriminating against or wilfully hurting other people, everyone should have the freedom to be who they are. Who we are is shaped by so many factors – our upbringing, our genetics and our experiences. We sometimes get so wrapped up in the present that we forget this when someone is acting differently, or is a little out of sorts.

The beautiful thing about people accepting you for who you are, warts and all (figuratively I mean – I don't have warts and I've no idea what the 'all' would refer to), is that your quirks and your flaws are accepted whether they're attributed to Asperger's Syndrome or not. Some of my friends don't know that I have an autism spectrum disorder or am bipolar. However, all of them know that I might have to cut off conversation to take five minutes now and again, or that I struggle in some crowds, or that I take things very literally. They know that sometimes I can get very quiet and down for long periods of time, and they know to give me space.

Keep in mind that you tend to attract people based on what you are, not what you want. In terms of being on the spectrum, this may mean that you tend to attract friends who are on the fringes of society, the eccentrics, the mavericks. This is a wonderful aspect of AS – when you're a little different yourself, you tend to attract those who are a little different too. Keep these people close – they will act like a mirror and will help you learn that it's cool to be different, that standing out in a crowd is a good thing, not a bad thing.

While I'm very conscious that being different can definitely be a boon, that isn't to say I walk through life all bright and shiny all the time. Like a lot of people on the autism spectrum, I have suffered with chronic anxiety for a long time. Simple things like just walking into cafés and bars, being around people or walking down the street become daunting, challenging tasks. It is a malfunction of our natural 'fight or flight' response, our response to external threat. In an evolutionary sense, snap decisions about whether to run or fight at a moment's notice could mean the difference between life and death; simply put, the difference between becoming an escapee and becoming dinner. In the present day, however, predators are in short supply, but the reflex is still there. When anxiety comes into the equation, instead of worrying whether we're going to become food or not, we worry about more unlikely situations, like being randomly attacked walking down the street, or more trivial situations like whether we'll say or do something that breaks an unwritten social code. If you're on the autism spectrum, there will undoubtedly have been situations where you've offended someone without realising it, or broken some conversational ethic without realising it existed in the first place. These situations make anxiety a lot more 'real' for someone on the spectrum, and often it feels as if the opportunity for social faux pas is ever-present.

I digress – what does it mean to be anxious in the first place, and how does it present? Anxiety, at its roots, is defined as the sensation of nervousness and worry about something with an uncertain outcome. However, anxiety in psychological terms goes deeper than this; the anxiety doesn't necessarily stem from the idea that the outcome is uncertain, the 'uncertain outcome' is replaced by a plethora of imagined situations, and the mind has a tendency during times of heightened anxiety to jump to the 'worst-case scenario'. This kind of worry activates the fight or flight reflex. Suddenly, walking down the street becomes a possible attack situation, a simple conversation can be tantamount to being eyed by predators, and entering a room can be like walking into a lion's den. When the anxiety becomes more severe, as characterised by generalised anxiety disorder, for example, your breathing starts to quicken, your heart starts to race and you may start to sweat. You can be irritable and on edge, concentration can become nigh on impossible. If not curtailed, this can quickly turn into a panic attack, causing hyperventilation, palpitations, loss of reasoning, abject terror and a sensation of impending doom. Afterwards, this leaves you feeling completely shattered – your body's supply of adrenaline has been expended, your muscles are tired and aching.

As an adult living with Asperger's, you're very likely to struggle with anxiety at some point, if not live with it constantly. This doesn't mean that you can't live a normal and healthy life, or a normal and unhealthy life if you prefer – this chapter isn't here to talk about your diet and lifestyle. Now I think about it, you can live a strange and healthy life if you want, too... Anyway, before I go off on a tangent, what I mean, is that if you deal with it in the right way, it doesn't have to stop you doing the things you want to do. There are a number of ways to deal with anxiety, and there's bad news and good news.

- **Challenge yourself:** I'll get the bad news out of the way first: one of the best ways to deal with anxiety is to throw yourself (tentatively throw yourself? Maybe throw is the wrong word) into situations that you struggle with. By this, I don't mean find the nearest club night when you're struggling with crippling anxiety. The trick is to school your mind, by repeated experience without negative outcome, into realising that a certain situation doesn't present any danger, or that the danger presented is far overstated. In terms of conversational anxiety, this can involve making a few mistakes. The key is realising that a social faux pas within conversation isn't life-ruining. Make sure that you do give yourself credit when you push yourself like this! Take it slow and steady and if you panic and have to leave, then that's fine. That doesn't mean you've somehow 'failed', it just means things got a little too much; there's always next time.

- **Take time out:** When I first started to challenge myself to enter into situations where I felt anxious, things would get too much and I'd leave. Then, when I was away from the situation, and I got home, on retrospection I'd realise I didn't really want to leave that much after all. At some point I'd go from being relieved about being away from the situation to wanting to go back to it. People with Asperger's are not inherently non-social. At some point during my late teens/early 20s I developed an innate fascination with people and the way they acted, their mannerisms, stories, hopes and dreams. This makes it all the more frustrating when I feel I'm held back by the symptoms Asperger's presents with, but makes me all the more determined to challenge myself. At some point, I started to think in terms that were a little less binary. A crucial piece of advice I learned for situations like the one I just described is that if things get too bad, then you don't always have to leave. When you get first go into somewhere, look out for the exits and keep it in your mind that you can always take five minutes out if things get too difficult. I went over this briefly in the chapter on employment, but it applies to many situations; if you have an 'out', take it when things get difficult.

- **Be self-aware:** Being self-aware is a key part of managing anxiety and can be something that people with Asperger's struggle with, as sometimes we can mix up or misread our internal messages or the urgency with which they present. I've gone for days without food because I wouldn't realise I was hungry, and wouldn't equate stomach pains with hunger. Other times I've become dehydrated, not equating lack of water with tiredness and dizziness. There is precious little research on this, but I know a lot of people with Asperger's who misread functional signals when it comes to the body. The reason I bring this up is that with the increased independence adult life brings comes the danger that these kinds of tasks will be neglected. This causes problems not just with general aspects, but with the emotional side of things too. When I forget to eat, I become irritable and anxious, and when I eat, that anxiety lessens or goes away. If you struggle to 'read' the signals your body is giving you, start to quantify how much you are eating and drinking instead. Make sure you're getting enough, as this does help. Besides this, try to look at what you're eating and drinking too. Now I see eating and drinking as 'refuelling' and I try to keep an eye on whether I'm getting enough vitamins, protein, carbohydrates and minerals. Try to moderate this – it's easy for this to become an obsession, and that carries its own problems. However, people often forget how intrinsically linked your mental health is to aspects of life such as eating and sleeping.

- **Sleep well:** There are many facets to the links between sleep deprivation and anxiety, some obvious, some not so obvious. Let's broach the obvious first. When you lack sleep, cognitive function suffers. Your reflexes take a hit, alongside your fine motor functions and core reasoning skills. There are highly documented links between sleep deprivation and anxiety disorders. In terms of Asperger's, this ties in fairly closely with self-awareness. When I was younger I used to misread the signs of fatigue and barely sleep at all. It became a vicious cycle; my body got used to the sleep deprivation, taking it as the norm. From a very young age, I got almost no sleep other than tiny microsleeps where my brain would shut down for brief periods. When you consider the brain as a computer, the links to anxiety become more apparent. The brain has to make an enormous amount of decisions to assess the danger in a situation, and if cognitive function is impaired through sleep deprivation, then there is a significant chance that it will misfire in doing so and misread a non-threatening situation as dangerous. In the same way a computer needs to shut down occasionally to maintain optimal performance, the brain needs to 'shut down' to recuperate.

- **Watch what you ingest:** There are certain substances that promote anxiety, whether found in food, drink or tablet form. Caffeine is a great example of this; it gives us an energy boost but also serves to speed up our respiratory and circulatory functions, increasing heart rate and breathing. By doing this it mimics and exacerbates the core symptoms of anxiety, adding fuel to the fire. Consequently, you're adding to your body's already overactive stress response. Start to monitor your caffeine intake and work on possible links between caffeine consumption and feelings of anxiety. If there is a correlation, then cut down the amount you're consuming. Remember, it's not just coffee that's caffeinated; tea still has three-quarters of the caffeine of a cup of instant coffee, and chocolate contains caffeine too. Do try to cut down gradually though, as it is an addictive substance and you may find you get headaches and shakes by way of withdrawal. Those symptoms will subside within a few days though. Of course, caffeine isn't the only substance that causes anxiety, though it is a big contributor. Other mainstream drugs, in particular alcohol, change the levels of serotonin in your brain and can cause anxiety lasting from around six or seven hours to two days afterwards. This is something to be very wary of with regards to the short-term relaxation effects of alcohol. Make sure if you have a drink to calm your nerves at a social event that you know when to stop, and do not become reliant on it.

Growing up with Asperger's Syndrome can be tough, and you can be plagued with anxiety and worry. Some of that anxiety is rooted in the fear of a lack of acceptance from others - fear that you won't be accepted for what you do, for what you say, for how you dress, even for the way you exist. There is a certain freedom to putting aside that fear.

As long as your actions aren't detrimental to the well-being of others, you should be free to dress and act as you wish. There's a wonderfully liberating feeling to existing without the need for affirmation from others, and it's somewhat contrary to modern social norms. Almost everything that is consumed, including the food we eat, the clothes we wear, the aftershave or perfume we buy and the places we inhabit, is carefully crafted to alter people's perceptions of each other. In this sense, people often consume things that are purported to make them seem individual. To a person with Asperger's, individuality is something that doesn't need to be adopted or acted out. It is something that in the first place started as a curse, an inability to fit in, the feeling of being a square peg trying to fit in a round hole. 'Aspies' are the mavericks, the free thinkers, we are the eccentrics. As we grow up, we have the opportunity to turn what was a curse in our childhood into a blessing in adulthood.

9
ANOTHER FINAL AND POSITIVE NOTE

NOW THAT YOU'RE CURED, dear reader, the time has come to get out into the big wide world and socialise. Go sow your social seeds. What's that, you're not cured? Good. The biggest key to growing up in the big wide world of adulthood is realising that you never grow out of it, and that if you somehow were to, you'd be missing out on a whole lot of good points. I'm not going to say that growing up on the autism spectrum doesn't get difficult, of course it does. In particular, as you grow older, you're gifted with a little more freedom and independence, and this can get pretty scary. There have been times I've wanted to throw my hands up and say, 'No thanks! I don't want it', and cast my adulthood back from whence it came. However, time waits for no one and unless you're Peter Pan, growing up is unavoidable. As an adult with Asperger's Syndrome or any other autism spectrum disorder, you have a battle ahead of you.

Don't worry unduly though, it's not all doom and gloom. As a child with Asperger's, I have to admit there were times that were pretty hellish. The process of 'fitting in', watching, listening to and dressing like everyone else was a necessity when I was young, but as the years pass by you start to be appreciated for your differences. Different is still cool. The key process lies in being comfortable with being different and challenging your personal boundaries. You can be viewed as a loner or outsider but if you make the effort to communicate, even with difficulty, and even in the clumsiest of manners, you will be respected for it. There is respect underlying the terms 'eccentric' and 'maverick'. Whether these terms are positive or negative depends on how comfortable you are in adopting this mantle, in being viewed as different. Be confident in this, and be confident in yourself. You're different, yes, but this isn't some defamatory adjective, some sleight, or even something to be taken lightly. To be on the autism spectrum is to achieve what every marketing director is trying to sell to other people – it's to be diverse, individual even. Take pride in that.

Autism spectrum disorders like, everything, have good and bad points. Like many people with Asperger's, I can become obsessive, wrapped up in one task or subject. This can lead to the exclusion of all else, even necessities like food and sleep. I need to be careful to structure my time when I'm working in a 'specialist subject' because of this. However, when I'm in the right mindset, I'm gifted with single-minded focus – I can be driven and directed in a task, only stopping when it's done. This focus is great, and I'm thankful for it. If a task that needs to be done crosses into something I'm passionate about, then I'm almost unstoppable – and I have a great deal of passion for my specialist subjects. This is something that a lot of people who aren't on the spectrum can struggle to muster, this unbridled joy found in certain subjects. It's incredible, euphoric even, and if giving up every detrimental aspect of Asperger's meant that I had to give up my 'specialist subjects' or obsessions, and the focus that goes with them, I'd refuse and shoulder the difficulties with a smile. Moreover, I don't think I'm alone in that sentiment.

A lot of people on the autism spectrum often struggle with expressing emotions – in general, if there is a problem we fix it, because that's more practical than a simple 'there, there'. Contrary to this, when it comes to a subject we specialise in, people on the spectrum can emote effortlessly. If you're on the spectrum, use this. Don't be afraid to be passionate, never be afraid to emote. If people aren't interested, then respect that, but if you can inject that passion into a conversation, you're halfway there. Just keep in mind that not everybody knows what you know, and not everybody wants to, but if you can be as passionate about somebody else's stories as you are about your own, I promise you, you'll do well.

As someone on the spectrum, your world view will be a little different to other people's. Of course, the core symptoms of Asperger's highlight the detrimental aspects of this. Social norms are strange territory, facial expressions seem to be in the realm of the extra-sensory, idioms used to make me feel like an idiot, and the crowds involved in parties and social events are just too much to take. It can be a little disheartening. However, there are advantages to thinking differently. As a photographer, I was constantly told that the perspectives I used were different, or portrayed things in a way my peers and tutors hadn't thought of. Even literal thinking has presented interesting new literary devices to add to songs and lyrics and new ideas for photos. It's a strange world out there, and often those seen as strange are just the ones who reflect on that fact. In addition to that, as the years pass, I'm more able to come up with lateral solutions to problems presented in day-to-day life, or even to highlight those that people have overlooked because they seem 'too simple'. The 'autistic world view' is something that can be as great as it can be difficult.

Just because people on the autism spectrum are different, and have a different world view on things, and often have the ability to hyper-focus, don't ever fall into the trap of thinking we are somehow 'better', or that our problems only exist through other people's perception of people on the spectrum. The problems that characterise autism and Asperger's Syndrome are very real, can be very debilitating and exist outside society's perception. When people on the spectrum blame their symptoms on those not on it, it propagates a 'them and us' rhetoric that has no place in an egalitarian society. In addition, to see people on the spectrum as somehow superior belittles the difficulties that people both on and off the spectrum go through. Be humble, as everyone has their own problems and everyone has their own strengths and weaknesses. If you treat everyone you meet as an individual, more often than not they'll respond in kind. Besides, everybody has some traits and mannerisms that lie somewhere on the autism spectrum. There is no blood test for autism; it is diagnosed symptomatically – those with a diagnosis only have enough of the symptoms to warrant one. When you oversimplify those on the spectrum as 'us' and those not on the spectrum as 'them', you (ironically, if nothing else) make things infinitely more complicated, and this can make diagnosis more difficult for everyone in the future. If this seems like I'm nagging, I apologise, but a more accepting and equal culture for both those with and without an autism spectrum disorder is positive for everyone.

I'm going to sound like a hippy here, but in a perfect world, people both on and not on the spectrum would be treated equally in that they'd be given due credence for their qualities and the acceptance needed to be secure in their faults. Everyone is human, everyone has their faults, and often when people are secure within them, they can become qualities that become endearing, a signifier of our unity in imperfection. If you are to have flaws, however, try not to let one of them be a quickness to judge others, with or without an ASD. Think back to the past, when you were judged, as we all have been at one point or another as adults. If you gift people with acceptance for behaviours you find different, they won't judge you so harshly if you exhibit behaviour outside the norm – and the chances are, you will come across as different sometimes. Use that, take those differences and make them your own. As a person on the autism spectrum, standing out in a world where many struggle to be seen is often not just easy, but natural. Be happy with that. Different is not just cool, it's liberating.

FURTHER READING

Attwood, T. (2008) *The Complete Guide to Asperger's Syndrome.* London: Jessica Kingsley Publishers.

Attwood, T., Evans, C.R. and Lesko, A. (eds) (2014) *Been There. Done That. Try This! An Aspie's Guide to Life on Earth.* London: Jessica Kingsley Publishers.

Bissonnette, B. (2013) *Asperger's Syndrome Workplace Survival Guide: A Neurotypical's Secrets for Success.* London: Jessica Kingsley Publishers.

Holliday Willey, L. (2014) *Pretending to be Normal: Living with Asperger's Syndrome (Autism Spectrum Disorder) Expanded Edition.* London: Jessica Kingsley Publishers.

Kim, C. (2014) *Nerdy, Shy and Socially Inappropriate: A User Guide to an Asperger Life.* London: Jessica Kingsley Publishers.

Mendes, E.A. (2015) *Marriage and Lasting Relationships with Asperger's Syndrome (Autism Spectrum Disorder): Successful Strategies for Couples or Counselors.* London: Jessica Kingsley Publishers.

Purkis, J., Goodall, E. and Nugent, J. (2016) *The Guide to Good Mental Health on the Autism Spectrum.* London: Jessica Kingsley Publishers.

Silberman, S. (2015) *Neurotribes: The Legacy of Autism and How to Think Smarter About People Who Thing Differently.* London: Allen & Unwin.

Simone, R. (2010) *Asperger's on the Job: Must-Have Advice for People with Asperger's or High Functioning Autism and Their Employers, Educators, and Advocates.* Arlington, Texas: Future Horizons Inc.

Steward, R. (2013) *The Independent Woman's Handbook for Super Safe Living on the Autistic Spectrum.* London: Jessica Kingsley Publishers.

USEFUL ADDRESSES AND WEBSITES

Ambitious about Autism
The Pears National Centre for Autism Education
Woodside Avenue
London
N10 3JA
UK
Tel: 020 8815 5444
Email: info@ambitiousaboutautism.org.uk
Website: www.ambitiousaboutautism.org.uk

Autism Research Centre
University of Cambridge
Department of Psychiatry
Douglas House, 18b Trumpington Road
Cambridge
CB2 8AH
UK

Tel: 01223 746057
Fax: 01223 746033
Website: www.autismresearchcentre.com

Autism Research Institute
4182 Adams Avenue
San Diego
CA 92116
USA
Tel: 866 366 3361 (toll-free hotline)
Website: www.autism.com

Autism Society of America
4340 East-West Hwy
Suite 350
Bethesda
MD 20814
USA
Tel: 1(800) 328-8476
Website: www.autism-society.org

Mind
15–19 Broadway
Stratford
London
E15 4BQ
UK
Tel: 020 8519 2122
Fax: 020 8522 1725
Email: contact@mind.org.uk
Website: www.mind.org.uk

National Alliance on Mental Illness

3803 N. Fairfax Drive
Suite 100
Arlington
VA 22203
USA
Tel: 703 524 7600
Fax: 703 524 9094
Website: www.nami.org

The National Autistic Society

393 City Road
London
EC1V 1NG
UK
Tel: 020 7833 2299
Fax: 020 7833 9666
Email: nas@nas.org.uk
Website: www.autism.org.uk

Index